PRISONER

OF THE

MIND

By

Jeff Hairston

Gantt Publishing Company
274 Center Deen Ave.
Aberdeen, MD 21001

Superwoman is Not My Name

I am strong, I am weak, I can be bitter or sweet,
but one thing about me that stays the same.
Superwoman is not my name.

Yes, I can handle many jobs and do them well,
give me responsibility and I won't fall.
So don't "dis" me or make me ashamed,
superwoman is not my name.

So you tell your friends "My woman's the best,"
then you invite them home to run a test.
If you want a dinner for twelve, you must be lame
because superwoman is not my name.

My family, I take care of because I love you;
not out of obligation, but the Bible says to.
But don't try to be lazy or give me a pain,
because superwoman is not my name.

Friends I do favors and solve problems galore,
but there comes a time 'I say "No more."
So try to understand, and please don't blame,
because superwoman is not my name.

I don't mind doing an honest day's work,
but when other employees don't it really hurts.
I am not a toy and I don't play games,
because superwoman is not my name.

Jesus, you see me when I am so weak,
you give me strength to reach the peaks.
Thank you, your love I proclaim,
You know superwoman is not my name.

– Cynthia Hairston, 2008 ©

Superman is Not My Name

I am the head of my house, a leader in my church,
but sometimes no one can see my hurt.
One thing about me that stays the same,
superman is not my name.

Yes, I can handle the stress and the pressure too,
sometimes all the responsibilities can make me blue.
So don't keep pushing me, or make me ashamed,
because superman is not my name.

So you tell your girlfriends "my man's the best",
then you invite them shopping to run a test.
If you want me to buy the whole store, you must be insane,
because superman is not my name.

My family I protect because I love you,
that's why I don't let you do the things you want to.
Sometimes I make wrong decisions that are a pain,
superman is not my name.

Friends I do favors and solve problems so fast,
but there comes a time when I have to pass.
So try to understand, and please don't blame,
because superman is not my name.

I don't mind doing an honest day's work,
but when I tell others they don't, someone always gets hurt.
Don't play on my intelligence, this is not a game!
Because, superman is not my name.

Jesus, you see me when I am so weak,
your strength and guidance I do seek.
Thank you, your love I proclaim,
You know superman is not my name.

– Cynthia Hairston, 2008 ©

ACKNOWLEDGEMENTS

Thank you to Claire Lesesne, of J&C Designs for the layout and formatting of this book; Editors, Ms. Pinson and Ms. Debra Heredia, and Proofreaders, Ms. Cynthia Hairston and Ms. Barbara Kramer.

Jeffrey Hairston,
Author, *Prisoner of the Mind*

The Prisoner of the Mind

In America today we have the largest prison population in the world, but how many men and women were locked up in their minds before they got to prison? What would cause a man or woman to sink to such a low place in life?

When a person's mind is clouded with all kinds of negative thoughts, those thoughts cause the person to take on a prison mentality, which is a place of confinement, a holding pattern. If the enemy wants to slow you down or bring your life to a complete halt, trust me, he will start by working on your mind. The mind is the seat of our emotions. What happens when we entertain thoughts of despair? These thoughts will cause us to overthink everything. If we want to feel better, we have to start thinking happy, positive thoughts.

I agree with the scientists who say you can't have a positive without a negative. That's true. However, Jeffrey Hairston says there has to be a balance. For example, imagine a car battery it has two posts, one negative the other positive. Take one of them off, and the car will not start because that is how the two work together.

Negative thoughts will definitely cause a downward spiral in life. I remember hearing someone say, "Look up and live." Maybe there is some truth to that saying. Looking up and not directly at the perceived trouble will lead you in the right direction.

When I was in the Army, my Drill Sergeant had a saying, which went something like, "Ain't no use in looking down cause ain't no discharge on the ground." We all have a bad habit of looking down when life deals us a bad hand. Can I be the first one to confess?

Looking down will cause you to go down mentally, spiritually, and emotionally. Here is an example of how life can throw you a challenge. What if someone goes to the doctor, and the doctor gives that person some bad news? Let's take a moment and think of it this way. What if this person is naturally a very happy person? People love being around this person and all of a sudden the doctor tells the patient that he or she has an illness that could be life threatening. What do you think the response will be? If that person accepts what the doctor says, nine times out of ten, the next time we see that "happy go lucky person," he or she will be in a depressed state. Why? The answer is because someone that the person trusted and believed in gave that person bad news.

The Bible says, "Laughter is like medicine to the bones." What if instead this person becomes joyful around happy people instead of hanging around the "graveyard" crew? Is it possible that over time, the body would heal itself? I think so. The grave is a place where all of us will reside one day, but if we spend our time around the grave, certainly we will get there much faster.

Bad news can make us walk right into a "jail cell" in our minds. We don't have to go to a "brick and mortar" prison to get locked up. The "lock up" starts as soon as we turn from the light and start looking at the darkness. In America, we have been taught that dark is bad. I beg to differ; darkness is only supposed to last just for a season, but some of us camp out there to prepare for the final bell. We must trust God to manifest in us the purposes and dreams that were predestined before the creation of the universe.

TABLE OF CONTENTS

TABLE OF CONTENTS

CHAPTER I

Nobody Can Hurt Like Me

The pain started when I was six years old. My teacher said "Jeffrey, recite your line in front of the student body." At that point, I felt fear like I had never felt before. During that moment, I started beating myself up with shame. I started shying away from the world. After all, no one ever taught me how to recite my lines. I was overwhelmed with fear. It's really amazing how some children can get up and recite their lines with no fear. It seems to come so natural to them. I believe most people start hurting themselves very early in life, and I would like to show some of the ways. Perhaps we together can shine some light on this epidemic called "low self- esteem".

Have you ever felt the need to prove something to someone? Have you ever thought to yourself, "I need to show them who I am"? While we are trying to prove something, no one is really looking, and that makes it hurt worse. I believe in a boy's life, the absence of his father can cause a huge void. It causes the boy to search for approval from others. If a boy is playing sports, such as football and basketball, and his father comes to the game, it makes the son play better because "Daddy" is in the stands. The father's approval does the boy's heart a lot of good. But, on the other hand, what if the father is not there?

I believe the son will start searching for a substitute. What is your substitute? What would you use to fill the void, and how do we spell relief? It goes back to the experience when the teacher asked me to recite my line. I, the child, felt insecure, but if Daddy had been there, maybe I would have had a sense of security.

I am just trying to draw a picture of some of the ways we as children develop low self-esteem and insecurity. I plan to talk a lot about "Jeff Hairston" in hopes that my story will help many others.

When I was around 11 years of age, I was so shy and fearful. I would go to dark places and hide from other people because for some reason I never felt as good as others seemed to feel. I remember once I went under the house and hid for about two hours. On that day, I really did something horrible. We had cousins visiting us on Sunday, and we were all playing together when I decided to roll this big rock down the hill where they were playing, and the rock hit my cousin in the knee. This is really why I hid under the house. I could hear everyone talking, and my cousin was crying at the top of his lungs. I wasn't about to take responsibility for breaking his leg, so I fell asleep under the house. Prior to falling asleep, I could hear everyone asking "Has anyone seen Jeff?"

I was right in front of their eyes. I could see their legs moving around as I crouched under the crawlspace of the house. They never saw me, but I could see them. I believe during this time of my life, I was developing a hide-until-it-all-goes-away mentality. Do you know that some things we create will not just go away? We must come out of the darkness and face up to our wrong. I think I hid that day until the sun started going down, and it began getting dark under the house. All of my family members started saying in concert, "Where have you been?" By this time they had already doctored my cousin and had come to the conclusion that his knee was not broken.

My question is, "Why do we have a need to run and hide instead of facing up to our wrongs?" Maybe we think it will hurt too bad to receive correction. Could it be that we have beaten ourselves up so badly already that the correction is just too painful? I'm just saying!

I'm writing this book in hopes that the readers can take something from my story that will help them avoid the pitfalls of hiding from reality. We live in a world where it's just not popular to be honest, which is why we have lawyers, that is if you can afford a good one in America!

We can lie, steal, cheat and kill; however, a lawyer will change the story for us and have us smelling like roses. Have you ever felt the need to lie rather than tell the truth? You don't have to answer this question. Just look straight ahead, and no one will even know it's you. Why do we hurt ourselves? Have you ever said this to yourself, "Man, I'm only hurting myself. I am not hurting anyone else. Leave me alone."

The question to ourselves should be: Why am I hurting myself; why am I cutting myself, why am I smoking cigarettes; why am I overeating; why am I drinking alcohol; why am I putting myself down? Well, GOD did not create us to participate in self-destruction! He made us perfect; we are created in the likeness and the image of the ALL MIGHTY GOD. He resides inside all of us. The air that we breathe is GOD. If you are not a believer in what I am saying, try holding your breath for ten minutes, and then tell me how you feel - if you live to tell me. Once conceived by our parents, we then were born by exiting the birth canal, and something happened. We opened our eyes to this place called Earth, which can be a little overwhelming at times, especially when the media day after day bombard our minds with fear tactics.

The sky is falling; the sky is falling! With all of that being said, my next question is: When will we stop hurting ourselves?

I decided two years ago that I no longer will cry about who left me, who dropped me, who did not treat me right. I'm moving on. We can spend our entire lives crying the blues! Why not get up and do something about the future? The past is the fuel that we should use to ignite the flame to propel us into our future.

CHAPTER II

Anxiety

Have you ever taken a test when all of a sudden your heart started pounding one hundred miles per hour? Your hands started sweating and you couldn't breathe? Maybe you were involved in a pool game, and, for no reason at all, here came these voices in your head telling you things like, "You can't win. Who do you think you are?" I'm really not sure what the psychologists call it, but I call it fear: False Evidence Appearing Real! I will be the first to testify that fear has almost robbed me of over half of my life. I recall once I had to speak before an audience. They told me two weeks in advance, so I had plenty of time to prepare, but something happened the closer the date came to speak. The voice of fear got louder and louder. Finally, the day of the event came, and I decided not to show up. How many people suffer from the same disease of tormenting fear? I am so tired of fear wrecking my life and regret the many times that I blew golden opportunities.

When I was in Germany, I was in the U.S. Army. My unit chose me to participate in a two-week mountain climbing event that I will never forget. We were ten to fifteen stories high on the tallest mountain in Germany. The instructor told us we had to climb the face of the mountain; then we had to repel to the bottom. Repelling is walking vertically down a fifteen-story mountain backward. I had to confront death face-to-face because one slip, and it could have been over. I was the lead climber when the instructor asked who wanted to go first. I was young, and when fear showed up, I would use the fear to my advantage. I would say things like, "If I die, let me die." Theodore Roosevelt once said, "Courage is not the absence of fear; it's the mastery of fear." I tend to agree with him because most people win scared. If we interviewed a pro basketball player, he would tell us that when he got on the court for the first time, fear was present, but he had to master the fear. The successful people in life all had to learn the same thing: to master their fear.

My question to the reader is: "How much longer will we allow fear to hold us back?" Ask yourself, "What good has fear been in my life? Has it benefitted me?" Then why do we keep allowing fear to handicap us? The questions should be: What is fear trying to block me from? Why does it always show up right when I'm about to reach another level of success? It always shows up to prevent me from winning. What does fear really want? Fear wants to label us as losers, but a winner will never quit, and a quitter will never win. One time a man was trying to invent a product, so he took his product to the market. They turned him away four hundred and eight times. I think I would have given up after twenty tries. This man decided to go back one more time. That's why he named his product "409." This is called persistence; we have to learn to be consistent and persistent. Never give in to fear.

We must learn the art of not quitting. Let the people laugh, let them talk, but don't give up until you win. Lighten up, fellow; it's not that serious. Most winners lose a lot before they win. Ask Michael Jordan. He was not the favorite in high school, but something happened when he went to college. The successful people in this world run to fear; the unsuccessful people run from fear. Running from fear will always keep us wondering what could have happened, or what should have happened. Are you tired of all of that self-inflicted pain? If so, then get up and do something about it. Take a deep breath and get back in the game. We are not the only ones that suffer from this disease. I am just crazy enough to confess that as big as I am, anxiety has played a debilitating role in my life. I am writing like a mad man trying to redeem the time. If a young person is reading this book, my advice to you is to start now at an early age overcoming fear. Get involved in as many programs as possible, at least the programs that challenge your fears. Join a public speaking group. Every time you stand up to speak, tell fear to release you. The more you do it, after a while it will come naturally. Finally, if you really plan to win, get rid of the scared people around you because fear breeds fear. Fearful people will only hold you back. Surround yourself with courageous people. They will challenge you to do more with your life. They won't give you a chance to sit around and drown in the pool of fear or anxiety. Millions of people have already drowned themselves in fear. Will you swim or drown?

CHAPTER III

Obesity

How many of us eat ourselves into a pit of despair? In the beginning eating seems to be great until the pounds start piling on. Then, for years to come, we live in denial. We begin to say such things as, "I am not fat." Everyone else can see it but us. Some of us will stand in front of the mirror and say, "I need to join an exercise class." But first, let us talk about what caused this excessive weight gain. One could be suffering from low self-esteem. Could we be eating to numb the pain, or should I say the self-inflicted pain? Could overeating from childhood cause scars? Could it be that we never really healed from the pain of a marriage ending? Could it be that we have been eating really to commit slow suicide, but just never had the nerve to get a gun and put an end to the pain? I was looking at the news the other day when a news flash came up. Depressed people often show destructive behavior. A woman in New York jumped out of her window from the eighth floor holding her baby. Surprisingly, the baby lived or the tragedy would have been much worse than it was.

So many of us inflict most of the pain on ourselves. Instead of crying out for help, we suffer in silence. Food has become some people's drug of choice, an addiction. These people need help. I am talking about self-inflicted pain. Carrying excess weight affects our hearts and our health, but it feels good to eat all of the junk food, right? America is over-weight, while some countries are starving to death. That's another subject I could start on, but I am now talking about obesity. I can't just highlight the problem without attempting to give a solution. First, we need to deal with the internal pain. Ask yourself some serious questions, such as, "Why am I killing myself? Whom do I need to forgive? Whom do I need to call to say I am sorry?" Ask yourself, "Did you quit on your dreams?" Sometimes we stop dreaming and don't realize it. Some of us need to find a life coach to help us work through the maze of obesity. Try taking a good look at yourself in the mirror. If you don't like what you see, then only you can change it. Never think it's too late.

The self-inflicted pain must stop somewhere. If you have this book in your hand, then GOD is trying to save your life. After identifying your pain and while you are resolving the issues, you also should try calling a gym to inquire about a membership. There are many to choose from: Planet Fitness, Bally's, Gold Gym, etc. We have to start somewhere.

I once had a fried named Willette Hurst who had a saying, "When you stop living, you start dying." Have you given up on your dreams? Only you can answer that question. If at times you feel like you are dying, then that's a good indication that you have given up on your dreams.

If you are able to hear me through this book, then stop right now with your self-inflicted pain. It's time to love yourself like you did when you were younger and slimmer. Do you remember how you looked then? Get that picture out and place it on your refrigerator, making a vision board of how you want to look. That same girl or boy is still in you calling out, "Save me, save me, save me!"

CHAPTER IV

The Color Complex

How many people have you met who were not happy in their skin? Who said things like, "I am too dark, I am too light, too brown or too red?" We see colored people wishing they were Caucasian, and Caucasians wishing they were colored. This is called a color complex. How painful it is not being happy with one's skin color? To be unhappy with our skin color is to say that GOD made a mistake.

When I was a child, people would call me black, and I developed a complex about my complexion. I truly understand how a person may feel, but again, I am writing to say, "Be happy in the color of skin that GOD gave you." How boring would this world be if everyone had the same complexion? GOD is a colorful GOD who loves variety! Let me talk a little bit about colored skin. For years other people tried to make colored ugly, and this caused a complexion complex, which caused colored people to waste money on bleaching their skin. Please stop wasting your hard earned money. Ironically, many Caucasians are tanning, trying to have a darker skin tone. The color of your skin cannot be so bad that you want to change it to meet someone else's expectations!

When we concentrate too much on skin color, that's when racism shows up to make our lives full of misery. There will come a time in life when we have to accept ourselves as we are. Try saying to yourself, "I am not too light," or "I am not too dark," and "I love me just the way I am." Think instead that GOD did not make a mistake when he made me. He made me perfect, and I am beautiful! Affirm yourself. Don't let anyone downgrade you any longer, and stop inflicting that pain on yourself. Today is a new day to be happy. Life is too short to cry about skin tone; the man in the graveyard wishes he had skin.

CHAPTER V

Letter to My Invisible Father

When I was a child, I loved to dress up in the middle of the week and my mother would say to me, "Your father loved to dress." I was too young to understand what she was saying at that time. She would say, "Jeffrey, you have sisters and brothers in South Carolina." My reply would be, "Mom, I have nine brothers and sisters right here." She would then laugh.

When I grew up, I joined the military, and something happened when I came home. My mother was sick with cancer and felt that she needed to make things right with me once and for all. She said, " I need to talk to you." My reply was, "What is it? Do you want to tell me that I have a different father than my other brothers and sisters?" She responded with, "How did you know?" My father was from South Carolina but lived in the Big Apple (N.Y.C).

Dear Daddy (Willie Gantt),

I sometimes wish that I could have seen you before you died. I believe you did love me. My mother told me that you did try to come and see me a few times, but both of you were married, so I understand. Did you love my mother? I have so many questions: "Is Art Monk, the football hall of famer of the Washington Redskins, my brother? I am asking because this is what I was told, but only you would have been able to answer that question. Daddy, why did you leave your wife in South Carolina? What did you want to be in life? Daddy, what stopped you from accomplishing your number one goal? Where is your grave? No one can seem to tell me. If I could see where they buried you, then the void that has been in my heart will heal. I love you, Daddy. I am proud that I have your picture. It really makes me feel good when I look at you in your Army uniform. I was in the Army as well. I made (Sergeant) E-5, and I bet you would have been really proud of me coming home after Basic.

My mother did a really good job raising me, and she told me so much about you. She said that you had a deep voice like mine. She told me that you were a very nice man and that everybody loved you in New York. I felt your spirit when I went to Manhattan. My friends thought I was acting strange, but I really did feel your spirit. My brother Willie Jr. told me that you used to go to all of Art Monk's football games with your cowbell. Did you love him? I met him. I went to his football camp in Virginia, and he signed your picture and shook my hand. Willie Jr told me Art Monk, the Hall of Famer who played for the Washington Redskins, was my brother.

I love you, Daddy. I met Gwen, my baby sister, and Goldie, my oldest sister. Big brother Willie calls me often. I am so glad that I had a chance to unite with them. Prince and I sometimes talk for an hour on the phone. I met Cousin Margaret; she is now 102 years of age. Her daughter Shirley told me everything about you. I always spend time at her home. Dad, I am letting go of the self-inflicted pain of searching for a dead father. It's time to let it go. I am a grown man now. I have written one book so far, and this is my second book. I will be a great writer someday. Daddy, writing this letter to you was suggested by my friend Tasha Jackson, who said writing would help in the healing process. Tasha, thank you. I feel much better letting go of the pain. Daddy, I love you. I don't hold anything against you; I understand life sometimes just happens. You got caught up, and my mother was a good one to get caught up with because we look so much alike. If I didn't look so much like you, I would not have believed Mom. I have to go, Daddy, but I won't stop until one day I put flowers on your grave. I love you, Dad.

Your son,
Jeffrey Gant (Hairston)

CHAPTER VI

Searching for My Invisible Daddy

I am a grown man, but deep down inside of me, I am searching for Daddy because I have questions that only my father could answer: "Why didn't you come to see me in Virginia? Why did you leave your wife in the first place? Why did you give up on your marriage?" These are questions that could never be answered, but I am writing to get it all out of me. You died February 1988, and I was discharged in March 1988, at Fort Devens, Massachusetts. (Wow!) Thanks to my cousin Shirley, I have been able to put some of the pieces of this puzzle together since I never saw you in life. I would love to see your gravesite. Shirley called the funeral home that buried you, and they gave her the right cemetery where you are buried. Soon I will be making a trip to New York to close this search. I really don't know what's going to happen when I see your grave, but I feel it will be life changing.

Why Do Some of Us
Quit So Easily?

I can talk about the Jeff Hairston I was when I was in the seventh grade during playtime. My teacher let the boys play tackle football; the opposite team kicked off to us. I caught the ball and returned it all the way back for a touchdown. I had a special gift for playing football. Next, when I got to the ninth grade, I went out for junior varsity. During practice one day, I ran the ball up the middle, and this kid hit me so hard that it felt like he broke my ribs. I started to quit that day, but I gave it a few more days. For our first game, we had on black and gold. Jeff Hairston was looking good. Everyone was in the stand cheering for Jeff, but the coach put me on the bench, and that's all I needed. At least, that was my excuse to quit!

Have you ever heard the saying "A quitter never wins, and a winner never quits?" Giving up and walking away has been part of my life since I was very young. I decided to write about the subject of quitting, hoping that writing about quitting will help me as well as help others not to give up so easily. I believe that when we quit, we leave too much on the table, which could possibly have us living with regret later in life, living with a lot of questions like "What if I had stayed? What if I had played?" I had a lot of self-doubt first of all. When the coach selected me for the team, I could not believe it. I thought he made a mistake. Here we go - low self-esteem showing up again! Young people, you must believe in yourself. Don't let anyone put you down and tell you that you cannot be what you want to be. Winners do over what losers are afraid to do over. Practice. Practice until you perfect the gift; after all, GOD gave it to you.

Please allow me to be your life coach. Get up and get back in the game. I wish I had someone to kick me in my behind every time I gave up. That's what we need; we need more life coaches to help young people to stop giving up on their dreams. After all, the dream is not for you anyway. It's for the world as a whole; every time we quit, we affect everyone around us. We leave people behind holding up what we

Why Do Some of Us Quit So Easily?

should have done. Aren't you tired of not finishing? Imagine a finished house! Sometimes, all we see is the construction site with boards, nails, paint, and bricks lying around, and this sight can be overwhelming at times. If you can somehow keep the picture of the beautiful finished home or work with the end always at the forefront of your mind, then maybe you can find the inspiration to not give up this time.

Have you ever sat around for hours pondering or worrying about life? Ninety-nine percent of us can relate to this subject. We worry about things such as, When will I die? How will I die? Will it hurt? Worry is a silent killer that most of us don't want to talk about. First of all, I can't write without talking about me. I plan to be as transparent as possible. The truth of the matter is that I am a worrywart. There have been times in my life when I have worried myself sick, and, most of the time, the worry was unfounded and self-inflicted.

Have you ever had a bill that was due and you didn't have the money, but you sat around worrying to the point that you could not sleep, lying awake at night worrying about tomorrow? I would like to confess that most of the time, I worried about a situation that was on my mind and would blow everything out of proportion. Can I tell you one thing about life? We have to decide either we are going to trust GOD or not. I once heard someone say, "If you are going to worry, then don't pray, and if you plan to pray, then don't worry." Can we say together that life is stressful? Say it again. Life is stressful!

We worry about things we can't change. Some people believe it's their job to save the entire world, but the entire world does not want to be saved. Tell me why do we try to carry the whole world on our shoulders? Can I tell you the truth? You cannot even save yourself, so stop trying to be GOD to everyone else. The people that care the most in life are the ones that end up with the load. Let me give an example: Just walk down the street and smile and watch how many homeless people come up to you and ask if they can borrow fifty cents or a dollar.

That's why most people in our major cities try to look mad but most of them are not really mad. They just know the game.

There's nothing wrong with caring, but sometimes we care so much that we handicap others. My grandfather used to say, "Son, every tub must stand on its own bottom." This is one of the old country sayings, and it's true. So often in life we try to help others when really what we are doing is hurting them. I watch parents do more damage in some cases than good. Mothers, you can't do everything for a boy and expect him to develop fully. It is so important that we allow them to fall sometimes. Let them play with rocks and dirt for a while until they learn to create. We were born to create, but most of us never get the knowledge that there is so much more in us. I have learned to stop worrying because worry is painful. I remember as a child I would sit around for hours worrying about when my mom was going to die. I loved my mother so much that I just couldn't believe she was going to die. Everyone someday will die, so now I look at how we waste time worrying about things we can't change. Maryam Rashadda Salaam was my mother's name. She died in 1995. My mother was my heart; she taught her children very well, and she loved everybody.

CHAPTER VIII

Trying to Please Others

Have you ever met a person who tries to be nice to everyone? By trying to make sure everyone is happy, this person wants no one to be upset. Some people make themselves sick by being people pleasers. They sacrifice so much of their own lives and years pass by. They find themselves in a rut. People have the wrong concept of how Christians are supposed to live. God never meant for us to give all of our blessings away and miss all of His blessings. I truly believe in giving, but we have to break the curse that says if you are blessed, you aren't humbled. The old saying says, "You must be broke to be humble." People who are going to love you will love you without your giving them everything. According to the words of Uncle Charlie Brown, of Havre de Grace, MD, "If you have to buy friendship, that's not friendship."

I believe friends should not lend each other money. They should give to each other because lending money can break up friendships. It causes friends to hide from each other when it's time to pay up. How many times have you loaned money to a friend, and they never paid you back? To avoid this self inflicted pain, just give the money to them. If it comes back to you, then to GOD be the Glory. Consider that a plus.

If you have to give all the time just to get along, then you need to change your circle of friends. Some people have the flim-flam spirit. They try to manipulate everybody, including their families, even their own mothers. Uncle Charlie told me that in this life sometimes we have to love people from a distance. It's not that you don't love them; it's just important that you consider who will get close to you. Most people will get close to you only to learn all of your secrets or to learn where your great strengths lie. They become busybodies in other men's and women's matters. Uncle Charlie would say, "Any dog that will bring a bone will carry a bone." Now I will bring that up-to-date. Anyone, who talks about someone else, will in turn talk about you. He or she has a gossiping spirit. To avoid all of that pain of being talked about, keep your business to yourself. Uncle Charlie said, "Where there is no wood, the fire will go out." In other words, where there is no gossip, conflicts cease to be.

CHAPTER IX

No Man is An Island

Isolation has become a norm in the last five to ten years as people seem to become more and more isolated from each other. Somehow the powers that be have decided that everyone should be separated. Ask yourself, "How does it feel being alone?"

I would like to try to draw a picture of how the world should be. Imagine the ocean. Have you ever been to a science museum where they show the ocean floor and all of its sea creatures? The fish swim in such harmony and unity, especially the tuna; we see millions or even billions of fish flowing together. What about the geese? Have you ever watched how they fly? They fly in order, usually one leader up front leading the way, and as they fly each one will break the wind flow for the other. It's only when we look at human beings, that we find so many trying to be islands. Once again, how does it feel to be alone? Really take a moment to think about that for a moment. Are we really following GOD's plan for our lives when we separate ourselves from the world? It's time to break the silence. It's a work of the devil to drive us away from our help.

There has been a calculated plan to divide and conquer. Take a look at our social media, like Facebook, Twitter, Black Planet and smart phone apps. We have traded our real family for an electronic family. Everyone has a profile with a picture and usually an old picture, or should I say a younger version of himself or herself. Everyone looks good online, but wait until you meet that person in real life. This is when you will hear, "Oh, I forgot to update my photo." That's funny, right? But it's true.

I watch people everywhere asking the question, "Where do I fit in life?" I want to warn you; we all were designed for a purpose, and until we find that purpose, there will be no fulfillment. But when we become islands, then here comes trouble. Loneliness shows up, and we will find anything to fill that loneliness. Some people fill it with drugs or alcohol; some people fill it with sex tapes or pornography. Some fill it with food, and before you know it, they have gained 100 pounds too much. Some people try to sleep the emptiness away and find themselves in a state of depression. The downward spiral proceeds. These are some of the things the devil tells us. He says things like, "She doesn't want you around; he doesn't want to be your friend." And we pass up our blessings, day in and day out.

The Bible says that he who finds a friend, must first show himself to be friendly (Prov. 18:24). Listen, my friend; we are all part of a bigger picture. We really need each other more than we can imagine. If we remain islands, then we will die on our islands all alone. I mean sometimes I can understand why some people choose to walk alone in this society because we have a lot of busybodies in the world. They love to be in other people's business and never take care of their own business.

Next, let's take a look at our major cities. We see homeless people being killed. It has gotten so bad that we watch people get killed in our streets almost every day. Everybody just walks on by as if nobody saw anything. When we become islands, we have all the violence that we see today. Would you agree that the last two young shooters that killed all those children in the school in Connecticut and in the theater in Colorado became islands prior to flipping out on the world? They were crying out for help, but no one could hear them. People are crying out for help, and most of them are looking for attention. We say we don't need the attention of others, but we really don't understand how GOD made us all. All of us are just part of the main. The main is the life source called "GOD," and GOD is love. We all need to be loved, and we all need to love. Have you ever been in a crowd of people, yet you still feel alone? This is called isolation. The devil is trying to set you up for the kill. He will tell you things like, "You are worthless; you are alone because no one loves you; no one wants you." But he is a liar. Don't listen to his voice any longer; get up out of that dry place and live.

Somewhere in this world GOD has a perfect fit, a place where someone needs you. In the beginning of this chapter, I talked about the fish. They swim in harmony because they are in their natural habitat. We should flow in love like a fish flows in water. Whitney Houston sang a song "Find Your Strength in Love." That's where our great strength lies. When we stop operating in love, we are just like fish out of water, and a fish out of water will eventually die. We will die if we don't find that flow of love, which is GOD.

.

Time to Get Focused on One Thing

Time to Get Focused on One Thing

Have you ever had a time in your life when it seems like millions of ideas will just flow into your mind at the same time? Better yet, have you ever met someone who has a million ideas about how to get rich, but she or he can't seem to get rich? It's time to get off the rollercoaster of life. Let's get focused for once in a lifetime. Life can become very stressful trying to concentrate on fifteen different things at one time. While we are trying to focus, life seems to pass us by with a lot of unfinished products. Here is what is really going on in our minds. I believe when we see too much at one time, GOD is showing us a picture of our future. We get excited and try to live in the future in the present, but the goal should be to take one day at a time or one step at a time. You see, Rome was not built in a day, not even in one year, so let's back up for a moment and start at step one by writing your vision on paper. Write it all down. I can now hear you saying, "Why do I need to write it down?" That is because it's not for you anyway. It's for the mass of people. Yes, what is inside of you is for someone else.

Just take a minute to digest what I said. Think about Sam Walton, the late founder of Wal-Mart. He started out working for K-Mart. Once he had learned K-Mart's system, he quit and opened a five and ten cent store. Here is his secret. He made a vow to GOD that he wanted to live off ten percent of his earnings and give ninety percent to charity. When he died, he was living off ten percent of his earnings, which was billions of dollars. He said, "Every journey starts with one step but some of us never take a step for sitting around looking at the picture." The picture can sometimes overwhelm us to the point that the excitement of it leaves us gazing and talking while others are focused on the goal. You keep wondering why for some people success just follows them everywhere they go. Someone said to me once, "It's the small foxes that destroy the vine." The small things compounded day by day will grow to be big over time. That's my interpretation.

Next, some of us have great ideas, but our problem is that we never get started, or we get started and then stop. We never finish one thing before we start something else - and something else. Think about this, what if your mom and dad had started and stopped when they were making you, where would you be now? They, at some point, had to finish. Aren't you glad they tried one more time? That's funny, but it's true. Somebody put some work in so that we could be born. It felt good, but it was not easy. Nothing worth having will come easy, so come on and push. Get focused! Start applying yourself just a little bit harder. You can do it with just one more push or one more pull. Let me put it in modern day language; don't stop, get it, get it! You understand that, right? To be successful will take the same drive and passion as making love. Your heart must be in it; if not, nothing will be conceived. Put your mind into it. Conceive it in your mind first and focus on the task, one step at a time. The Bible says, "As a man thinketh in his heart, so is he" (Prov. 23:7). So if you can think it, then you can conceive it. It's time to fight for your baby. Say to yourself, "If it is to be, it is all up to me. I am the master of my own soul. I am the captain of my own destiny." That is not saying GOD is not in charge, but GOD gave me a mind to create my own destiny. That is why he said, "So as a man thinketh in his heart, so is he." I think I am a millionaire or a billionaire!

We have so many people praying for blessings from GOD, and they are going about it the wrong way. We need to meditate on one thing at a time: get it in your mind. Think about it, talk about it, breathe about it, and get into it until you conceive it. Push, man, push! Women, your destiny is here. You dreamed about it. You saw it in the far away distance. Now the birth pains are coming frequently. Your baby is trying to tell you something: Push! Now give Him praise for all He has done. Amen.

No Pain No Gain

No Pain No Gain

Pain is a feeling triggered in the nervous system. Pain may be sharp or dull. It may come and go, or it may be constant. You may feel pain all over your body. Pain can be helpful in diagnosing a problem. In fact, pain sometimes can go on for weeks, months or even years; however, pain can be sometimes good or bad depending on the cause. When a weight lifter goes into the gym, the first thing he must do is break down the muscle for the first couple of days. All he or she is doing is applying pressure to the muscle, and this process can be very painful. A few days of breakdown may cause some to quit because it just hurts too bad. But give yourself about a week to heal. Now it's time to build. Isn't that what life is? It seems like we always have to endure some pain to get to the promise. So that explains why some never get to the promise. They can't endure the pain.

We walk through the gym, and we see guys and girls looking like the heavyweight champs of the world, but what price did they pay to get those triceps and biceps? Even after the muscle is built, in order to go to the next level, we have to start all over. We have to break down that muscle in order to cause it to grow to the next level.

CHAPTER XII

Looking for Approval

So many of us seek approval from others for various reasons. We ask questions like "Should I wear this?" or "How do I look?" I hate to inform you: we are all pre-approved. GOD approved us during conception. Did you know billions of sperm cells died, but you survived! When we ask for approval, it's a slap in the face of almighty GOD. Secondly, some people believe they were born wrong, or someone taught them that they were born on the wrong side of the tracks. I believe what the Bible says in Genesis, "Man was made in the likeness and image of Almighty GOD" (Gen. xx:x). That's exactly what we need to teach our children. If we teach them more about the mold from which they were created, it may cause them to act more like GOD. In fact, if what we have been teaching is right, then why do we have so much unfinished product? So many of our youth and adults can't seem to find a vision of who or what they should be.

When men or a women can't find themselves or don't know who they are, this creates a void in their lives as they seek approval from others. We ask questions such as, "Who am I? What am I about?" To say this may sound funny, but it's true. When a man does not have a clear self-identity when he makes love, in some cases he will ask the woman in the middle of having intercourse, "What's my name?" And the woman, like something crazy, will answer with whatever his name is. Ladies, what you have is a man trying to find his identity through sexual intercourse. Ladies, it's a man's job to tell a boy who he is. A father should lay hands on every son before the drug man can get a chance to lay his hand on him. I'm not going to leave me out of this story because I want to be transparent about my life.

I spent most of my life looking for approval. Don't get me wrong; it's good to have a mentor, teacher, parents and even pastors, but the final decision in life is between us and GOD. If GOD approves of us, then why do we look past GOD and ask people for approval? When we ask people what kind of day they may be having, they may give us advice based on how they feel at that moment. To be honest, some people are outright jealous, and they may give you bad information because they don't want to see you succeed. Or they want to control you, so they can take credit for your success. They may say, "I taught you everything you know," or "Without me, you would be a nobody." You set yourself up to walk right into that trap the moment you start asking or seeking approval. Followers are usually the ones who get caught up in situations like this. Also, some people would rather ask others for advice so that they don't have to take responsibility for their own actions. Can I tell you the truth? The most talented people sometimes fall into this trap because they fear being hurt and because of past hurt. The hurt won't allow them to step out on their own for fear of being rejected.

I will be the first one to say rejection doesn't feel good at all, but until we learn to deal with rejection, especially in this day and time, we have to say to ourselves, "So what?" and move on. Most of us allow others to wound us over and over again. We go home and get depressed instead of laughing at that fool and realizing that winners will always get rejected. But it's important that we don't give up. Jesus was rejected, so who do you think you are if you don't understand that rejection happens to everyone? It's time to get some tough skin or to go home. This is what we have to do in 2015. A lot of people are sitting on the sidelines waiting for someone to give them a job or bail them out. Well, what if they don't get bailed out? Then they get the hell up and bail themselves out! Don't forget we were created in the likeness and image of Almighty GOD. GOD is in every creature. We are all different in the manifestation of our Creator, so stop acting like losers. It's time to win. Yes, I said it; you have what it takes inside of you to win. I know you think it is too late, but did GOD tell you it was too late? If you can still hear GOD's voice speaking to you, then follow His instructions and let Him lead you to your promised land. He approved you at birth; now start acting like your GOD. Start thinking like him; stop putting limitations on what you can do or whom you can be. You can have and do whatever you want to do. I will see you at the top, or I will see you from the top!

Chapter XIII

Destroyed by a Double Mind

Many of us have experienced times in life when we just couldn't seem to make up our minds, but eventually we came to a conclusion. But what about the time we made up our minds to carry out a particular task and changed our minds thirty minutes later, or some event or someone helped us change our mind? The Bible says, "A double-minded man is unstable in all his ways." How has your unstable mind affected you in this lifetime? Well, I can tell you about me. I should be a millionaire by now. I allowed so many million-dollar ideas to slip right through my hands because of starting and stopping. One day I was up, and the next day I was down. I confess my faults. The Caucasian man has no control over me. All my life Jeff Hairston has been living with a double mind, telling myself things such as "Jeff, you don't qualify for the task." No Caucasian man did that; Jeff did it.

I believe confession is the key to my healing. I never felt good enough. One mind would say, "You can do it Jeff;" and the other mind would say, "You can't succeed." The negative mind defeated me for so many years. I am now writing not out of defeat, but I'm writing out of victory. I will recover. Soon I will stand before thousands and declare to them, "You can make it!" My low places in life have prepared me for my high place. Every time I allow the enemy to talk me out of my blessing that is the same level that I will destroy his kingdom because I experienced it firsthand. Oh no, it's not over; the fight is just getting started. I am getting ready to move from the back to the front. I have been a back seat rider for too long. So move over; you might be in my seat. I am taking my mind back: Single minded. It is what it is.

Chapter XIV

Think Big and Get Big

How many times have you made yourself look small to try to prevent others around you from having the feeling of being small? Well stop it! After you made yourself feel small, the other person may not feel big at all. You just wasted time and energy on someone who has a small mentality. No more shrinking to make others feel big! If others cannot accept you as a big man or woman, drop them and walk alone until GOD sends you the right crowd.

Some people want you to shrink down to make them look good because when you walk in your true self, you walk in light. Sometimes there is too much light in a dark place, so people begin to tell you that there is something wrong with you. If you believe them, then you become their darkness. Ask yourself a question; what if Michael Jordan had made himself small to get along with people?

We must start today. We must create a new society of young people. We need to affirm them day and night until they start to believe that they are special or they have value inside of them because that is really where the value is: on the inside. We have power going to waste in our youth today. If you look around, everyone has a cell phone, but have you ever considered what the cell phone is doing to society? It makes people handicapped. How? I am glad you asked! GOD gave all of us minds, but we are trading brainpower for computer power. I am not against computers, but I am against the dumbing down of children. They are not learning to think for themselves. Man is trying to create a computer that will take the place of the human mind, but the problem with that is the computer doesn't know right from wrong. GOD gave us minds so that we could learn the difference between good and evil.

It is time to see yourself as GOD sees you. "Lord how do you see me?" I believe He will say, "I see you as a GOD, one that has creative power." The Bible says in Proverbs 23:76 that as a man thinketh, so is he. What we think daily is shaping our lives. What have you been thinking lately? Well, we must begin thinking like our GOD thinks.

And how is that? GOD thinks without limitations. So why do we think with a limited mindset? It's because we think too much with our flesh mind, and we need to start thinking with our spiritual mind. In the spirit there are no limits. In the spirit we can have what we say, for life and death are in the power of the tongue. So speak life daily; wake up and say, "I am that I am."

I can do all things through Christ that strengthens me. I have power to destroy the enemy of my soul. I am a millionaire. I have everything I need, and I can have, be and do anything I want. I am wealthy, I am healthy, I am a king, and I am a queen. I am the head and not the tail. I am a wealthy businessman or woman. All of my accounts are running over with money. I have money to give away to others. Now that you have affirmed yourself, get up and move out of that apartment. Get the house you always wanted. Get the brand new car that was promised to you; get out of that relationship, and find yourself a healthy relationship. Now I will see you at the top!

What do you see when you close your eyes? We call it imagination, but could it be GOD showing us how beautiful He wants our world to be? Look at the flowers and the bees flying from one flower to another with a scent of rain in the atmosphere, the wind blowing slightly, the children playing hop scotch and jack rock. Do you remember when we were children, and we would play all day? Then, around 5:30 p.m., we would hear a bell, and all of us would take off running to catch Mr. Frosty and get that big cone of ice cream. Could it be that GOD wants us to remember when we were children and to stop taking life so seriously? Maybe GOD is saying, "Let me be Daddy; I got you covered, son or daughter." So go play; some of us need to have a let's-just-play day where we get out with the children and act like one of them again. Being too serious can cause high blood pressure and could cause a heart attack or stroke. Don't be so serious; everything you have been worrying about will soon fade away.

When I was younger, there was a song called Don't Worry; Be Happy. The song would say something like this, "In your life you will have some trouble, but when you worry you make it double." This is what happens to all of us. We magnify our problems by worrying, and the problems become giants in our lives. Yes, we need to throw the stuff we sit around and worry about overboard and go to sleep. I did not say go to bed because most of us go to bed, but we lie there awake looking at the problem. Worrying is like the alcoholic who tries to drink his problems away. When he sobers up, the problem is still there, but now it is worse. Help is the magic word here. Most people have too much pride to admit that in life, at one time or another, we all will need to cry out for help.

CHAPTER XV

DARE TO DREAM

Let Go of Dead Things

Have you ever been stuck in a situation where everything was dry, but for some reason you decided to stay there? I understand why so many people allow themselves to get stuck in dead situations; it's because of perceptions. Could you imagine a child living in a place where dysfunction is the norm? Then how will he grow up to be an adult and break the mold of dysfunction? This is why we have rap artists rapping about the hood. The hood is what the rapper perceives. One day I was in a poor side of town. All of a sudden, I started feeling depressed and hopeless; despair was trying to creep up on me. Then I got in my car and drove to a rich side of town. All of a sudden, I began to feel hope and creativity. GOD has a place of hope for all of us, but some of us love to hold on to dead things, and dead things will kill our spirit. It is dead; then bury it!

This is why we have so many people in our mental hospitals. Most of them have dead situations in their minds. Whatever died doesn't want to let go. They don't want to let it go and move past that point. Next, have you ever tried to focus your mind and the more you try to focus, these dead things start talking to you? Stuff that should have been buried years ago is still hanging around. Maybe you had an abortion, got a divorce or lost a job, and you just can't seem to forgive yourself. You are not alone. Mental problems are an epidemic. I have never seen so many people walking around talking to themselves and talking to dead things. Some people may lose a loved one, and twenty years later they may still be stuck at the day of the death.

However, I can't talk about this topic without attempting to give a solution. First of all, we must come to grip with the reality that in life we will lose people and things. We have to accept the fact that one day all of us will die. Stop for a minute and ponder that. If we know this, I believe we should live every day like it is our last day. Tell someone, especially your family and friends, that today you are dealing with depression. Maybe for some reason you can't let go of the past.

Let Go of Dead Things

Don't waste the rest of your life living in the past. Maybe your past was painful, but GOD can heal you if you let Him. Find a support group, one where you can share your pain with those who have experienced the same or even more tragic situations. Your past does not have to become your future. The enemy wants to destroy your life by trying to hold you in a place of "unforgiveness." I know it hurt, but we can't go back and relive our pasts. It drives some of us crazy because we are unable to go back to this one way ride.

My friend, let's start making the best of it because we are wasting life crying over spilled milk. The Bible says, "All things work together for the good of them that love the Lord" (Rom. 8:28). I did not say everything in our lives have been good, but when we mix the good with the bad, as my grand-father use to say, "Take it with a grain of salt." GOD can take all of our broken pieces and make something great. If we ever want to express the greatness in all of us we have to let go of dead things, wipe our tears and look to our bright future. We manifest in life what we think about. Could it be possible that we are creating our own hell on earth because that's all we see or have seen in the past?

It's time to get another picture in our mind called a vision. Ask GOD to give you a new vision for your life. Go out and buy yourself a vision board. Put it on your wall at home. Place it somewhere so that you can see it everyday. Write on it where you want to go, where you want to be in ten years. Cut out some pictures of your dream home, your dream car, your dream husband or wife. Whatever it is, put it on the board. Place on the board how much money you want to make. The universe is wealthy, so don't play GOD cheap. I will see you at the top. Peace.

If you want your "Yes" to mean anything, you have to say "No" more often.

We Say Yes
When We Should Say No

We Say Yes
When We Should Say No

Once an old man told me never to say "yes" when you are happy. To me at this age now, that saying goes against all logic. But now after living a few years, I understand what he meant.

When we do say "yes," it ought to be after we have weighed all the facts. Most of the time most of us say "yes" without knowing the facts or the repercussions of that "yes." How many times have you allowed someone to smooth talk you into saying "yes" and years later you wish you had said "no"? Parents do it all the time. "Mom or Dad, can you take me to practice on Monday?" We reply "yes." Then Monday comes, and we have to work late, which causes a conflict. Let me help you out. The world loves people who do not know how to say "no," and they will use the hell out of you until you stand up and say "no." It's okay to just say "no." It's not a bad word. People just want you to feel guilty. Some people say "yes" to get approval or just to get along with others. I guess we can call it peer pressure. We allow people to pressure us into situations that we know are not suitable for us at the present time. Then, afterwards we feel guilty.

We say such things as, "I knew I should have said, "No. I loaned my last dime to him or her." Why did you do it? You did it because of your own low self-esteem. You felt that just maybe loaning the money would make a person like you more, but money can't buy love or affection. So, take it from me: Get some tough skin and learn to say "No." Secondly, if I were you, I would just adopt the word "no" for a while until you get yourself together because all of those "yeses" have you in the mess you are in right now. Really, it's okay to share as long as others share alike. This world has a lot of users, and they seek out the weak or the meek.

I hate to say this, but women suffer the most from saying "yes", especially if they are dealing with a no-good man. For example, the guy may ask for sex, and the woman will say "no." The guy may take that as a "yes," but she may say "no," then give in by saying the one word that will get her in big trouble for the rest of her life. She has to live with, "Why did I say 'yes'?" The bottom line is that any "yes" needs to be considered. We need to weigh the cost before we say "yes" because it may cost us more than we can afford to pay.

Get Off the Merry-Go-Round

How many more times will you tell your friends about that problem? How many more times will you tell yourself about that problem? When we stay on that merry go-round of life, it will eventually make us sick and tired of being sick and tired.

Sometimes in life we commit ourselves to situations that are impossible to maintain, or we get tied up with people who are not moving forward. It's very important that we surround ourselves with the type of people that challenge everything inside of us. We need to surround ourselves with those who refuse to let us become comfortable with less, we need people who will tell us the truth, even if the truth makes us mad. There is a common saying, "Friends don't let friends drive drunk". People who are drunk don't usually want to hear that, but it's the uncomfortable truth. The questions we all should ask ourselves are very important: Who are my real friends? Are they the ones that make me mad, or the ones who make me happy?

When I was in the Army, my drill sergeant used to make me so mad that I really had ideas a few times of killing him during that moment, but after the eight weeks was over, I began to love my drill. I realized he was hard because he loved us, and most people run from what is hard. But the hard stuff in life is what molds and shapes us. When I took a good look at my body after eight weeks, I was in the best shape of my life. I then began to say such things as, "Thank you, drill sergeant, for conditioning my body."

Most of us may run from the drill sergeants of life. They may come in the form of a doctor who may say to us that we may need to lose weight due to health reasons that can lead to heart conditions. We end up walking out of the doctor's office upset instead of accepting what was said. We continue to maintain obesity, and then develop high blood pressure and diabetes. Remember, your friends who will tell you the truth are your real friends.

Get Off the Merry-Go-Round

I may not agree with a totally free society because so many people will do what they are big and bad enough to do. Nobody can tell them anything, so they get on the merry go-round of life. However, if most of us would listen to the warning signs of life, this world would be a better place. Now we are going to talk about getting off the merry go-round. If it were easy, we would not have so many people on it. Usually, when we try to disconnect from a system, job, or a person, we have an anxious feeling of "What will I do next?"

CHAPTER XVIII

Everything Should Flow

There have been times in life when I had to encounter many roadblocks. Some were set by others, but most were set by myself. First of all, let me name some roadblocks: lack of education, fear of the unknown, fear of success and fear of public opinion. Then we have doubt, disbelief, procrastination, laziness, obesity and religion, just to name a few self-inflicted roadblocks. Maybe we can identify with some of them because some of them have been added to our lives, or almost destroyed our lives. My main purpose for writing this book is to assist someone with the realization that it is possible to learn from other people's mistakes. We live in the richest nation in the world, so the excuses that we make are lame. We say things such as, "I can't find a job," or "They don't like me." However, I believe everything in life should flow. Take a look at the fish in the ocean or the geese in the sky. My question to you is, "What's your excuse?"

How Bad Do You Want It?

Chapter XIX How Bad Do You Want It?

Let's see what Webster's Dictionary has to say about the word "want." To want something means "lacking or equal to requirement, absent or not supplied." Have you ever wanted something, and for some reason what you wanted just wouldn't manifest in your life? You waited and waited, and after a while, frustration and doubt set in. First of all, you will start doubting yourself when other people step in and start saying things, such as, "Man, how long do you plan to wait? Your husband or wife is not coming," or they could possibly indicate that the money you are expecting is not coming.

When we have wants in our lives, want is another word for need or lack. What happens if what you want you really need in your life? What if the want is supplied? Then would your life move forward? Want is the worst type of emotional pain one could ever suffer because what you want could really be a need. The enemy wants to try to block our blessings from manifesting in our lives because he knows that if we ever get what God has promised us, so many others in our lives will be blessed. Our lives are connected to millions, and that's why for all of our lives our wants have been the major stronghold in our existence. The very thing that we have been wanting has been all around us. And that made it worse because we had the possibility of being able to see it and almost touch it, but for some ungodly reason it seems like someone is blocking us from receiving what we really need.

Ask yourself: How long have you talked about the things you want? How badly do you really want the need fulfilled in your life? Do you want it badly enough to go after it? I believe that after waiting a long time for something to come, if it doesn't hurry up and come, then you should pack your bags and go meet your blessings. Say to the blessing, "Since you didn't come to me, I decided to come to you." To want something is really saying that we have a need that went unfulfilled, and it hurts too much to continue to want it. In this world we have too many people who want but can't seem to figure out how to get what they want.

Ask yourself this question: What is it that I really want? Many people want freedom, but when freedom takes a long time to come, it begins to work on the mind. The plan that God has is that we all be free. God never planned for His people to be in bondage. The enemy's plan is to make sure "want" continues to be part of your life.

I have watched people year after year live a life of "want" to the point that some have lost their minds wondering how much longer; some have given up completely and committed suicide, some by spiritual and some by physical suicide. I have watched women sit around and wait for a husband for ten and twenty years, and they want a husband so badly that it has caused them to give in to any man, knowing he is not the right one.

I have watched others give up on their dreams, but deep down inside they want to do better. What is it that you want and what's really stopping you from going after what you want? I want to be transparent for a minute and talk about Jeff Hairston. I have desired to be a millionaire for years, practically all my life. I desired to be rich. I dreamed of having a school in order to teach students different trades, such as tractor trailer driving, barbering and cosmetology. I also dreamed of having a bank named "First Minority Savings & Trust." But can you imagine having all of these dreams locked up inside? Wanting something for a long time without getting it can drive a person insane, if you know what I mean. Some of us are forced to sit around and watch other's dreams come true because money is offered to them freely, affording them the opportunity to manifest their dreams, while others can't seem to even get started with their dreams. As a result, they end up living a life of want.

No one can tell me that a mother of three children living in an apartment doesn't want something better, or the man working every day to support his family doesn't want more money or a larger home. When we get into the wanting and waiting room of life, we have questions. The questions are, "When" and "How much longer will I have to wait?"

Maybe someone is trying to block it from coming, or maybe God is upset with me. After all, I don't really deserve it anyway. We may say something such as, " If God provides me with the things I really want, I won't be able to handle it; maybe I will go back on my promises to God. After all, why should God bless me anyway to be a millionaire?" Or, "No one else in my family has ever been rich. As a matter of fact, most of them are poor." Next, "Why do some people receive everything in life, and it seems like others can't break the glass ceiling of poverty." I am glad you asked. The Bible says: As a man thinketh in his heart, so is he (Prov. 23:7). Could your negative thoughts be the main cause of your slow or no manifestations? Could it be possible that because our minds have been programmed with all of these negative and self-inflicted, destructive, critical, low level, doubtful and faithless thoughts, they are the harvest of our minds? Since the Scripture is true, then how can we manifest anything positive when our minds are attracting nothing but negative fruit?

One time when I went to the doctor's office, I told him that I wasn't sick. I just made an appointment to have a heart-to-heart talk. I shared with him that I wanted to open a state of the art salon and spa. I wanted aqua water massages, barbers and hair stylists. In the same building I wanted a health spa with exercise equipment, such as bicycles, tread mills and nutritional drinks. I said, "Dr. Halstatt, every time I make up my mind to start the business, two things stand in my way: (1) a lack of capital, and (2) something in my mind continues to talk me out of it. One day my mind tells me I can do it, and the next I feel unqualified and unworthy. My doctor looked me straight in my eyes and said, "Jeffrey, what you are fighting is a negative mindset. He said what you have is a great idea. You should step out and do it. When you have your grand opening, I will be your first customer." That was ten years ago, and this negative mind is again about to cause me to miss out on something great. "As a man thinketh in his heart, so is he" (Prov. 23:7).

Some people understand the power of the mind, and they train their children in a positive mindset. They teach them never to think negatively about themselves. They teach them to walk around with their heads high. On the other hand, what about the child who has to break through the abuse of hurtful words spoken by mothers and fathers, or hurtful words spoken by other family members? These words could consist of, "He's not my child anyway; You are just like your no-good father; He wasn't anything and you won't be either." These hurtful words can travel with you for a lifetime. They can cripple you from going after your dream. Years can pass you by, and you will find yourself in the same place, just talking about your dreams while not being able to get over the hurt.

Antoine Fisher said it in the movie *Who Will Cry for the Little Boy?* He decided to make a movie about his pain in order to help millions of others who may be or have been suffering the same trauma in life. This is exactly what I am trying to do: expose my childhood pains to the world in hopes my story will help children and adults all over the world to get over their pain and manifest their dreams.

My goal is to write my way out of the darkness. The more I write, the better I am beginning to feel about myself. I have always struggled with feeling good about myself because my entire life has been all about how others felt about me, rather than how I felt about myself. That's a lot to deal with in one lifetime. My story is one of many, and just like Antoine Fisher, I am defeating all those who tried out of ignorance to defeat me. I want it bad enough now to forget those things that are behind me. I have decided to reach for those things that are before me. I am pressing forward towards the mark for the price of the high calling, which is in Christ Jesus.

If we hold on to our past, our past will hold on to us. But when we confront our past and deal with the hurts one at a time, they have to release us to fulfill our God-given destiny. My advice to the reader is: Release those who hurt you. Forgive them because they didn't know you were a king or a queen in the making. There is a king in you; there is a queen inside of you. The world needs to see what has been hidden inside of you. We are all diamonds in the rough for the most part. Look! I can see the diamond starting to shine. You may still have some rough edges, but your day is coming. Never stop dreaming. Can you imagine the glory that is about to be revealed in you? They called you the underdog by saying you wouldn't make it. If you want something badly enough, you will stay up late and stay focused for as long as it takes. Get some help; cry if you have to. Do whatever you have to do, but don't quit. Don't let want destroy you, but go after what you want. Be like Michael Jordan. Just do it.

The emotion of want I believe is one of the main reasons or causes for depression. When we allow want to fester in our lives too long without going after what we know we should have, it becomes a cancer that starts to eat away at the center of our soul. I believe God created us to create our own world, but what if we never learn the secrets to creation? We end up walking around and around wasting life. What a waste to waste the gift of life. The secret to manifesting what we want is in our thoughts. The Bible says that as a man thinks in his heart, so is he focused. Thoughts create in the natural what we see in our spirit. Frustration comes when we can hear and see greatness on the inside and poverty on the outside. I am determined to enlighten the masses of the people by writing it in a book. Please hear my heart. You must break free from what's holding you back. Ask yourself, "Is your future worth wasting?" Think about it. Who will be lost because you lived a life of want, but you didn't want it bad enough to go after it. No one is blocking you but you! It is you telling you those lies in your head, telling you things like, "It's too late for you; you don't have the skills, and everyone else is more qualified; you are dumb and stupid. "Stop listening to your head for a moment and start listening to your heart."

So much is depending on your success. Millions are waiting on you to step up to the plate. There's no one else in the world that can do it like you. God is calling you, which is the reason why you have been waking up in the middle of each night at the same time. Every night God is saying to you, "Don't miss your season." Too many people are hoping that you succeed in life to let them down. I know the enemy has been telling you that everyone is against you, but everyone hasn't gotten to know you yet. As soon as you come from out of hiding, the whole world will know you. Look at Tyler Perry and Steve Harvey. They came from the bottom to the top. These guys have great testimonies on how they went against all odds. Even sister Oprah, she was a small time reporter in Baltimore, Maryland, but you see her now. She has her own show and even her own network, the Oprah Winfrey Network (OWN).

Chapter XX

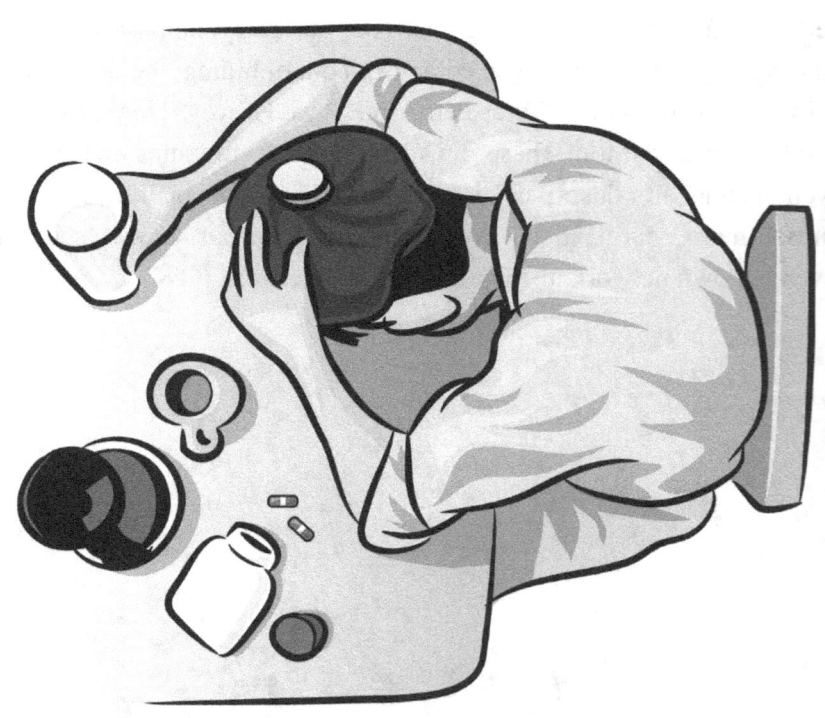

Self-Medication

Self-Medication

First of all, I am nineteen years clean from drugs and alcohol. However, I am only now starting to heal from what made me an addict. In the beginning of my addiction, I was around 13 years of age when my brothers and I stole one of my father's Old Milwaukee beers from the refrigerator. I can tell you my addiction started that day because I traded low self-esteem for a temporary high. I felt so good that day that when the high wore off, I wanted to steal another. I think I found heaven in a bottle, so when I turned a little older, we moved to a larger city from the small town of Ridgeway, VA. I then started to experiment with black beauties, blue and clears, windowpane, paper blotter (better known as acid), hash, and marijuana.

My addiction started with one beer. At the beginning phases of my addiction, it was fun until I started hallucinating. Next, I joined the U.S. Army, and by then I was a full-grown addict. When I went on leave to my hometown in Virginia, I met a girl named Valerie Still with whom I feel deeply in love. Little did I know she was already involved with a man named K.T. Turner! However, she told me that she was single. Next, one day when I went to her house to drop her off, I had an encounter. KT had his hand on his gun in his pocket. I was in the Army, so I was bold. But I wasn't stupid. I walked around my car and raised the hood of my car. His response was "What is wrong with your car?" I was beginning to get nervous. I was face-to-face with death. Next, because I was afraid that he was going to shoot me, I went around to the trunk of the car and took out my tire iron. I was acting like I was checking my tires, but really I was about to knock his brains out with the tire iron.

I guess the prayers of my mom kicked in at that moment, because he looked at me and said, "This time I am going to let you go, but the next time I see you with her, I promise you I am going to go off." I felt "what a relief!" I escaped death once again.

I left that scene and drove right back to her house, picked Valerie up, and took her to my sister's house to drop her off. She was saying, "Why are you dropping me off?" I could not tell her that I was on my way to a friend's house to buy a gun. I wasn't about to get caught again empty handed. After all, I was Uncle Sam's property, and they taught me to kill! I purchased a 22 revolver. Remember, at this point in my life, I was a 22 year-old fool on the move. I was driving a candy apple red Trans Am with tinted windows. The gold bird was on the front of the hood on the car, with me and the gun inside.

Now let's back up for a moment while I tell you how I received the tags for my car. I was an expert dice shooter, so prior to leaving from Fort Riley, Kansas, I was at a dice game in my friend's room, and I had the hot hand. I took just about everyone's money in the dice game when this young man whom I knew was broke was in the room. So I began to tell him how I needed tags for my car. I offered him $40.00 to buy his. He agreed and proceeded outside to his car, where I made the purchase.

I then drove fifteen hundred miles from Fort Riley, Kansas to Danville, Virginia with another man's license plates on my car. I just thought I should add how I got to Virginia; I was on 30-day leave en route to Germany.

One evening, Nick Wooden asked me to race him, saying he would blow the doors off of the Trans Am. So I took him up on his offer. We started in Martinsville, VA, at the red light. The first one to Ridgeway would win. I was running 140 miles per hour when something happened---- my steering wheel came off of my car. But to top it off, the state trooper was behind me, and I had the nerve to have a gun in the car. I had left Nick so far behind that I didn't even see him.

My heart was in my throat when the steering wheel came off. I decided to outrun the police. I put that steering wheel back on just enough to continue to drive, starting with a quick left and then another. The trooper thought I went straight when I lost him once again. Another day in which I escaped death!

At this point my sister told me I would not live to be thirty, and she was right if I had no acceptance of Jesus Christ as my Lord and Savior. No doubt, my mom would have lost me to those streets. God delivered me from a horrible pit. No matter where you find yourself, give your life to Jesus. I know if he can save a thug like Jeff Hairston, he can do the same for you. I am grateful today that I am now living one day at a time.

Give a Man a Fish,
Feed Him for a Day,
Teach Him to Fish,
Feed Him for a Lifetime

Give a Man a Fish, Feed Him for a Day,
Teach Him to Fish, Feed Him for a Lifetime Chapter XXI

In America we have a lot of native Indians, some on reservations, such as the ones in Arizona. The U.S.A considers reservations restitutions, but I would beg to differ. Most Indians probably agree that alcoholism plays a major role on the reservations. This is because giving someone a free lifestyle can be as harmful as slavery to the mind of a slave.

Also, in America we have a welfare system set up for those who fall on hard times in life. The system is not bad, but the act of giving free food without teaching a man to get his own food can cripple the man beyond recovery.

Have you ever seen a child who wants to leave his or her parents' home if he has been given everything he wants? I believe one of the reasons is that the child has gotten comfortable being fed from hand to mouth. In most cases the child doesn't have the will to survive on his own due to years of being programmed to be dependent by loving parents.

I suppose this same process happened during slavery of the Afro-Americans. Those in slavery stayed on the plantation in the South working for the slave master, eating his food. This taught them dependency when his counterparts were taught to be independent.

Slavery was supposed to be over, but the problem with the slave is he was never taught how to free himself. This is why we have so many dependent people on the system in America today.

Look at our prison system, which has the same process that the slave master used to enslave the minds of the slaves. When we put a man or woman in a cell and house that person for so many years, providing them with three hot meals and a bed, it's no wonder that when they get out, in ninety days or less they will return to prison. During slavery, the masters never taught the slave to be self-sufficient. They were beaten if they were caught trying to excel by reading. We need to create a new system in the world, adopting a new way in which we can teach all to fish.

Give a Man a Fish, Feed Him for a Day,

Chapter XXI   **Teach Him to Fish, Feed Him for a Lifetime**

Let's discuss what happens to us when we eat for free over a period of time. Something inside of us will die because God created men and women to create. We are born to create just like God. How do we create? We create by the thoughts we think. God has placed a vision inside of his people, and that vision needs to grow. This vision needs to be expressed in society. We handicap people and rob the entire world of the gifts that are locked up inside of the dependent persons. America, your ancestors robbed the slaves and millions of people are being robbed now. What is really inside of the ex-slaves in America? Could it be possible that you enslave the kings and queens of Israel? If so, greatness is inside the African race. America is suffering due to many ex-slaves being taught to depend rather than to defend!

The greatest investment in this world is to invest in the African culture. So much has been locked away for too long, and one of the biggest mistakes American has ever made was the slave master sending the slaves away without restoring them with an honest attempt, since I see the "feed me" mentality in a lot of people.

I was raised as a child in the Nation of Islam. We went to the temple on Saturdays and learned so much in the F.O.I. Elijah Muhammad gave us hope, and I have never seen such unity. The Nation of Islam taught us to share whatever we had and provided help to those who needed it. Unity is the key, with men and women uniting from within themselves in order to learn how to unite with others.

Stand Still and See the Salvation of the Lord

Stand Still and See the Salvation of the Lord

Sometimes in life trouble just seems like it won't go away. Have you ever been in a storm where it seemed like no matter what you did or how much you prayed, your life stayed the same? I heard so many people say things like, "Just pray, brother" or "Just pray, sister." But have you ever prayed and nothing happened? I spent years praying, and I will be the first one to say, if all of my prayers were answered, I would be a millionaire or even a billionaire. I had a sister whose favorite line was, "Somewhere in my future, things look better than they look right now."

Have you ever met a person who looked really good on the outside, and it seemed as if he or she should be sitting on top of the world, but for some unknown reason, he or she was sitting on the bottom? Could it be possible this person could suffer from mental problems, confusion or low self-worth? Before you start judging, get to know the person first, because you really don't know her or his background or the roadblocks this person has had to overcome due to traumatic experiences in life. I recognize that I am making a lot of inquiries, but this chapter is designed to challenge your thinking. Have you ever felt caged, yet you were not in a cage? Have you ever felt like a loser even though you have given your all to win? What about the feeling of sorrow in the middle of the day for no apparent reason? Do you wonder why these overwhelming feelings of sorrow come over you? How about when your heart starts to get a little heavy? Could it be possible you are facing imprisonment within your own mind? How long have you had this mental imprisonment? How long have you been looking through those invisible bars, smiling and laughing, but deep down on the inside you feel like crying? You are not alone. If you look around, you will find millions of people who are in prison with you. It is a shame that we have physical prisons that handle criminal behavior, but we don't have mental prisons that can incarcerate negative thoughts and help people with their lives. We have more people living in their own mental prisons than we have in our prison system.

The people who are incarcerated mentally walk around every day with feelings of low self-worth. How can we stop the mind from saying negative things since the only person who hears these voices are you and you alone? Some people call those voices demons. I call them the voices of lies. Most of us have been taught so many lies in our lives that no matter how much truth we hear, the lies just keep talking. It's time to block the lies and time to believe the truth about ourselves. How can we believe the truth when we have all of these competing lies? They told us that Santa Claus came down the chimney. They told us the Easter Bunny lays eggs. God only knows how many other lies they told us! I am here to tell you the lies were designed to put us in a mental prison. If someone lies to you, that lie becomes a curse to you because the lie has you doing everything in reverse. How many of us were lied to as children? Maybe someone called you stupid and you ate that lie that now lives inside of you. Maybe the lie of not being human, which was told to our ancestors, is still living in you. It will take another two hundred years to reverse these lies told to African-American people. As President Obama said, "Man, we been bamboozled."

CHAPTER XXIII

Wait on the Lord

Take a good look at your life. How many times have you walked away too soon when you were so close to reaching your goal? I have found one thing out: Life has a way of making you wait, especially when it's something worth waiting for. I believe that once we accept the fact that no one is going to give us anything, we will get in line and stay in line. Experience has taught me to stay in line since I started trading stock. I have learned so much about waiting. I bought so many companies and held them for a while before I decided to sell them. As soon as I sold the shares, then all of a sudden the price of the shares would go through the roof! I guess most of us have walked away from things that we should have stayed with. Experience is a good teacher! However, wisdom is the best teacher. The Bible says: If a man lacks wisdom, then let him ask God, and He will give all the wisdom that you may need for a lifetime. Wait on the Lord; *He shall renew their strength. They shall mount up on wings like an eagle; they shall run and not get weary; they shall walk and not faint.* (Isaiah. 4:81)

Because that's what God does!

Chapter XXIV

Knowledge of Self

To thine own self be true.

When you have a slave's mind, he will automatically go to the back door.

We undercut other men when we don't know who we are.

The measure of my Manhood: I am man enough to admit when I am wrong.

Protect – Provide – Teach

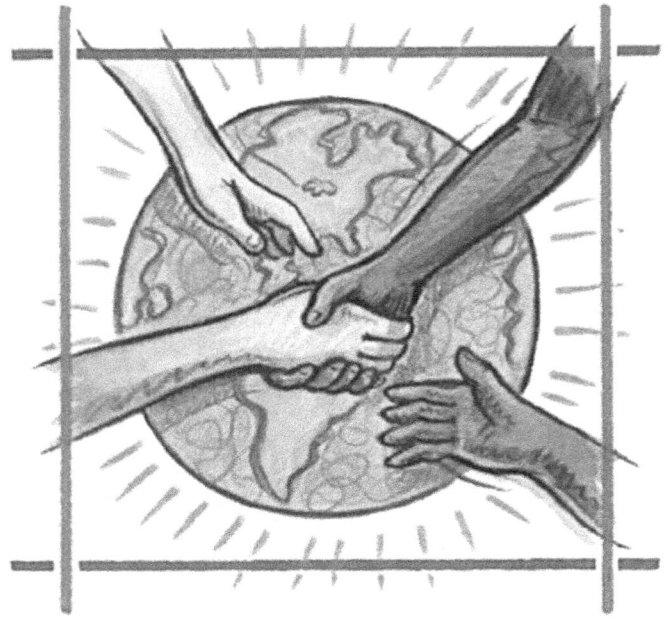

This is a Quote by Uncle Charlie Brown

This is a Quote by
Uncle Charlie Brown

Jesus said to love your neighbor as yourself, but he didn't say to love your neighbor better than yourself. He told the rich young ruler to sell what he had and give to the poor, but he didn't say give it all, so we need to come to a positive understanding of what He really did say. People get confused because the preacher teaches them to be confused. Let's talk about Uncle Charlie Brown from downtown. This man will run you out of the pool hall, but I forgot to tell you how old he is. He's seventy-nine years of age. Uncle Charlie has a lot of wisdom; he said he used to be confused and thought he was supposed to give everything away to the poor, but where would that leave him? So many people give away all of their money and end up with nothing. Uncle Charlie also said he went to church once and wore his yellow shirt and nice two-toned suede shoes. The preacher preached her whole sermon about how much he looked like the world. Thank God that we have graduated from those days because God wants us to educate ourselves and not be dumb.

LOVE
YOUR NEIGHBOR AS
YOUR
SELF

Depression

Depression

The World Health Organization estimates that 121 million people worldwide have some form of depression, with less than 25 percent having access to effective treatment. According to the National Institute of Mental Health, about 14.8 million adult Americans experience clinical depression in any given year. Webster's Dictionary defines depression as a severe despondency and dejection typically felt over a period of time and accompanied by feelings of hopelessness and inadequacy. Jeff Hairston's definition of depression is years of unfinished business. When we are born, God places a destiny inside of us, but why do some and not all people carry out their destinies? Could it be that life turns us around with its ups and downs and changes along with the hurtful things done to us? Some individuals carry resentments that become enlarged in their hearts. This causes them to ponder day in and day out the hurts of their pasts.

What about resentment? Resentment is having been treated unfairly, holding on to the cancer day after day, year after year. Is it possible that most of our unfinished business is our inability to forgive? Depression is years and years of baggage stored in our heads like a computer that has to be cleaned from memory. So do our minds need cleaning? Computer attachments, emails, spam and other items enter our computers daily, and most of us never empty our trash. This allows electronic Trojan horses and viruses to cause the computer to slow down or even crash because of unfinished business. Over the years, our souls have attached to unwanted email that is in our heads. We hear voices of gloom and doom, voices calling us losers. Maybe the confusion is coming from all those emails in our heads that we never deleted. Could our spam boxes be full?

Everything given to us in this lifetime has to be maintained. Could it be time to clean up our houses? How many of us, when cleaning, sweep things under the rug? That's the same thing that happens when it's time to clean our computers. Viruses try to hide under the rug. Could it be possible depression is the result of years of unwanted programs running in our heads? Well, it's time to clean your house. It's time to close those programs and delete all those that take up space. Am I saying a person can defeat depression once and for all? Yes, but it won't be easy.

I suffered years of depression; some days out of nowhere sadness or gloom would appear, and sometimes I would give in to it. Once I gave in, there went the rest of my day. From that point, I would try to find a dark room, usually my bedroom, where I would give in to depression. I would hear voices advising me that I would be better off dead and telling me to take my life. Agreeing with the voice made me transparent enough to speak about being there with others who are unable to tell anyone. Why do we have so many people committing suicide? They hear the voices telling them to take their lives. If they told people about these voices, people would start looking at them as weak. No one wants to hear or be looked upon as weak. Everyone wants to appear strong, especially men.

In writing this book, I am hoping to break the silence of the lambs, I want to break the silence of the wounded warriors. Even warriors need a place to bleed. Don't keep walking around acting tough in front of people and crying in silence, ashamed to talk to people about what's really going on. I am talking about me. Can I be honest? I carried years of depression because I would never deal with what was eating away at me. If something were wrong, instead of confronting the problem, I would suffer because I never wanted to see others suffer. I would hurt for them. How crazy does that sound? The word for this is called co-dependent. To be free from co-dependency, we have to be honest. After all, why waste an entire life trying to be something that we are not. It's time to delete all unnecessary files. I am not waiting until New Year's. Most of us never stick to our resolutions in the first place. We should ask ourselves: why would you love others more than they love themselves? The Bible says we should love our neighbors as we love ourselves (Matt. 22:39). First, we have to love ourselves. How can we give someone else something that we don't have? Love is the power from which we should all operate. Abundant love; God is love!

Veterans and Depression

Chapter XXVII Veterans and Depression

When I graduated from high school, I was looking forward to the big day to board that plane and head to basic training. I was really proud to be a soldier in the U.S. Army. I served seven years with three tours, one in Germany and one in Fort Devens, Massachusetts and Fort Riley, Kansas.

Going back just a little, let me tell you about my experience at Fort Dix, New Jersey, where I spent eight weeks in basic training. When I first arrived at Fort Dix, I was as green as they come, a country boy from Virginia. But after eight weeks of running four and five miles a day, low crawling and jumping in and out of the foxholes, the U.S Army had taught me how to be a man. I would say the Army was successful in changing a country boy into a broad- thinking man. After all, all I had ever seen were the little old towns of Danville and Ridgeway, VA. I was in the Army riding high on a cloud. At least, that's how it felt to me. The Army made me believe that I could fly, and on days when we didn't feel that we could fly, we had a team of people that gave us positive reinforcement. Basically, the Army took my mind to a place where we were not allowed to think for ourselves. The Army had a 24-hour schedule for us to follow every day.

This is where the disconnect comes in. When I left the Army after seven years, there was no one to tell me when to get up or when to go to bed. Now I'm looking around, and it's hard to find anyone who wants to work together as a team. Could it be that the Army sets veterans up for failure by putting us in a teamwork environment for so many years, making us believe that the Army life presented is how life really is? The Army sends us home, and all we can do is look back and remember our battle buddies. Our battle buddies are the first people assigned to ensure that we always had someone to watch our backs. Then we come home and run into a bunch of cutthroats! I am not badmouthing the Army; I am just trying to shine some light on why we have so many depressed veterans. There are millions of soldiers walking around looking for a mission to carry out as a team. Since I left the Army, I don't think there has been one day of my life that has passed without thinking at some point in the day about my glory days as a soldier. The world had a certain level of respect for the green uniform; then when the mission was over, we came home only to get disrespected and, in some cases, racially profiled.

Take a look around at our veterans hospitals. Veterans are coming home missing arms and legs, depressed, suicidal, homeless, suffering pain in knees and back; we paid a great price. Some even lost their lives for freedom. We went into foreign countries and stayed away from our families for sometimes two and three years, only to come home to a world that doesn't have any idea of what kind of price we paid. So many veterans come home with blood on their hands. What do I mean by that? We were all trained to kill. I never killed anyone, but I know those who killed. How do they get those pictures out of their heads?

Chapter XXVIII

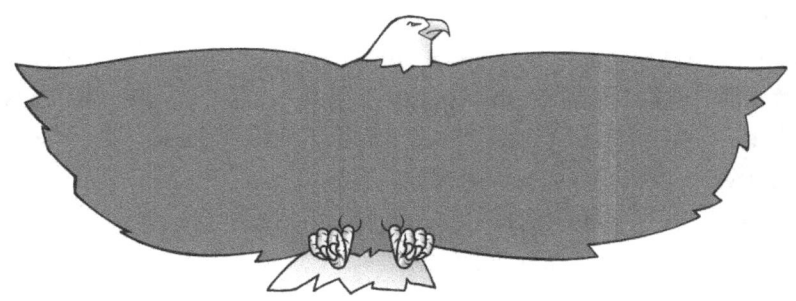

Eagles and Chickens

I would like to pose a question. What makes eagles hang out with chickens? Could it be the eagle has been trained to act like a chicken by hanging out too long with its lower counterpart? Could it be that the eagle doesn't know it's an eagle? That's what happens to an individual when he or she hangs out with people who think on a lower level. They tend to adapt to that environment. We live in a society where we lock men and women in cages like animals. Can you imagine what that feels like? A human being who has an unlimited mind locked away for a few years or even life. I once was locked up in the county jail for five days. Those five days felt like a lifetime because I never understood the concept of prison. Even though some people are so out of control that society has to put them somewhere to protect society, what we have is a lot of unfinished product. What a waste to have a 16 or 18 year-old walk up in front of the judge only for him to say "life without the possibility of parole."

Society would rather lock people away and not deal with the real issue. My questions are: What are we really dealing with? What causes a person to choose darkness over light? What is it that causes human beings to fear light? John 3:19 says, "Man chooses darkness over light because his deeds are evil." However, what happens when a man wants to bring his evil to the light? Society says that when he, comes clean, punish him. I remember when a track star won a gold medal, but she used steroids. She decided to come clean. But after she confessed, they gave her six months in federal prison.

CHAPTER XXIX

How to Overcome Fear

What is fear? Breaking it down, fear is false evidence appearing to be real. The thing that has been chasing you is not even real; it's only a shadow. Do you remember when we were children and they used to say things like, "Boy, you are scared of your own shadow?" There's only one way to overcome fear. Step 1: Ignore the feeling. I took public speaking in college and discovered that everybody, even the President, gets butterflies when he speaks in front of large crowds. Janet Jackson confessed that she had stage fright. The secret to overcoming it is to do the act scared until the fear goes away. The Bible says, "…to stir up the gift that is within you" (Tim. 1:16). What does that mean? It means whatever the enemy is trying to stop you from doing, do it even if you feel the emotion of fear.

CHAPTER XXX

Stop Believing Lies

It's not what you believe that stops you in life but rather what you believe that's wrong. That is what can hold you back in life. For example, for many years we believed Santa Claus was real, and many believed that he came down the chimney even though they did not have a chimney. For years, we believed the Easter Bunny laid eggs until we found out the truth about Easter. Easter images came out of Greek mythology. There was a Greek goddess of fertility. You get it? Eggs (Fertility)? If you want the truth, then you came to the right place. I don't plan to waste your time giving you a pack of lies. The title of my book is *Prisoner of the Mind*, and lies are major tools used to enslave the minds of the masses. Just in case you are not in agreement with me, ask yourself this question. Could falsehood be the invisible force field that has held you down all these years? The Bible says, "You shall know the truth, and the truth shall make you free" (John 8:32).

Since God has given me the grace to write this book, I may as well tell the truth. When we study Greek mythology, take a look around the world. All we see is Greek mythology from the White House to the church. I don't see why I should waste time writing without telling the masses the truth. Alexander the Great went to Egypt and conquered it, but after he conquered, he took over the royal libraries. They took the knowledge of Egypt and established a country called Greece and decreed that all knowledge should come from Greece. If you don't believe me then go out and buy a 1611 King James Bible and try to find a "J" in it. The reason you can't find a J in that version of the Bible is because until 1637 there was only twenty-five letters in the English alphabets, and in 1637 they added a J. Jesus walked the earth two thousand years ago. I will let you research the rest to find out what his real name was on the cross.

Next, I believe most of us spend years learning lies and have to spend years trying to unlearn those lies in the same way. Too many of us eat ourselves into the person that we don't want to be until the day that we wake up and realize we are fat. Then we spend the next ten years trying to get skinny. When we believe lies, this is the beginning of our downfall in life. In the present day, it's very hard to find people who believe in truth, which is the reason I screen books before buying them to avoid reading about lies.

What if you woke up one day and found out you were a king, but all of your life you were told that you were a slave boy. Would you even know how to act in the palace? This is what is wrong with most African Americans. We have been lied to. Someone said Blacks in America were only sixty percent man and we believed that lie. But now, how could we be 60 percent human and our ancestors built the pyramids in Egypt. The Rosetta Stone came out of Egypt and without this stone we would not have language. The Caucasians brought our ancestors over from Africa and beat them into submission. They then told them they were animals because to not be human makes you an animal. Could this be one reason why our prisons are loaded down with African Americans Most people know that what I am saying is true. I often wonder why everyone else knows who we are, but we continue to walk around in chains. I am sounding the alarm. It's time to take off the chains. No, they are not natural chains; they are chains of the mind. You see, in order to chain a nation as strong as our people, first they had to be chained psychologically.

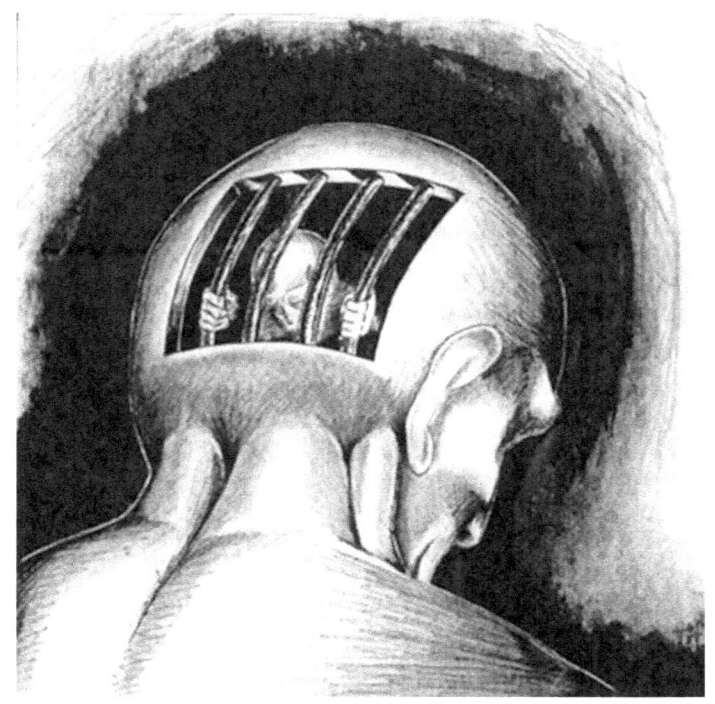

CHAPTER XXXI

Psychological Slavery

First of all, slavery comes in many forms, but slavery of the mind is the worst form of slavery. The Emancipation Proclamation was signed in 1862; however, the African in America is still not free because it takes more than a signed proclamation to set a person free. Now, this next statement may cause some people to walk away from me, but it has to be said. Religion was the tool used to enslave the African, so it's kind of hard to set someone free with the same Scripture used to enslave. The slave masters used some of the same Scriptures that we read today. Let me give a few examples: Slaves obey your masters or you will be beaten with many whips. They also the nerve to say, "Thus saith the Lord" after using the Bible to justify slavery and cruelty. Secondly, the slaves were not allowed to read and now that we can read, we are discovering nuggets like, "So as a man thinketh, so is he." If a slave wasn't allowed to read what could he really think about? He had no way to learn and advance and demand his rights as a human being, and he also had no way to write to tell his story to future generations. His mind was trapped in this dark night of oppression. So the phrase "So as a man thinketh, so is he" was working in reverse because the slaves' minds could only reproduce pain, suffering, fear and confusion.

I often wonder as an African American if we will we ever see justice served to the Africans in America. My question is to the enemies of African American progress what are you afraid of? Why do you work overtime to continue to make laws that are designed to hold the African in an inferior position? I was raised as a child in the Nation of Islam. Yes, at nine years of age I was in F.O.I learning things like who is the original man? The original man is the Asia Attic Blackman who was the maker, the owner, and the cream of the planet earth. The earth is ninety three million miles from the sun. Light travels at the rate of one thousand and one third miles per second. The earth weighs six sextillion tons a unit followed by twenty-one zeroes. Those are some of the things I learned. As a child, I really felt empowered until my teacher, the honorable Elijah Muhammad, died suddenly.

However, today I am a Christian even though I often look back on the days of unity in the nation of Islam. We were taught self-sufficiency and knowledge of self. It took me a while to understand what the honorable Elijah Muhammad taught us. He was trying to raise the self-esteem of a people from believing we were animals because the whites had written laws to govern animals, not humans. Muhammad was trying to reverse the lies that were drilled in the minds of the slaves. He knew that you can release a man from physical chains, but until the man is released from psychological chains, the man will remain an animal in his own mind.

Dr. Martin Luther King Jr. said in his famous speech:

No lie can live forever; truth across the earth will rise again; this is the hope that we must stand on. When God got ready to deliver the children of Israel, he shined the light on a man named Moses and told him to tell Pharaoh, 'I said let my people go.'

God is raising up great men and women who see the need to teach in a way that the curses of the mind can be purged from the minds of His people. I believe 2014 will be a year of deliverance for descendants of slavery. God is concerned about our freedom; Mandela said people are not free until they are economically free, but Jeff Hairston says people are not free until they know the truth about themselves. Then, and only then, can they learn to build an economic foundation.

CHAPTER XXXII

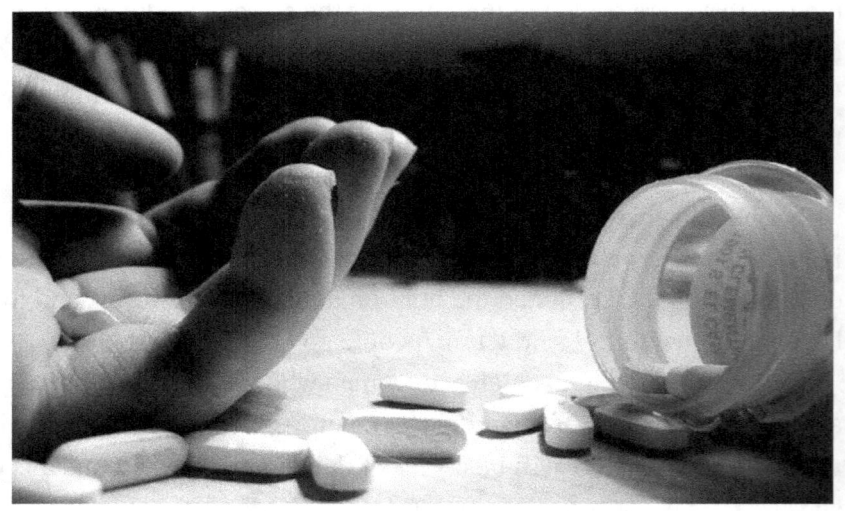

Suicide in America and Abroad

Studies show that most people who committed suicide never sought professional help. Between 1952 and 1995, suicide in young adults tripled. Suicide is the 11th leading cause of death in the USA, and at least 750,000 people will attempt to take their lives in one year. My question is: What is it that could cause a person to want to end his or her life? Some people, especially religious people, will first say the devil is on the loose. Yeah, baby, that old devil, but how much is, or should be blamed, on the media and society with its negative announcements daily? First of all, I want to say the Bible does say that the devil is the author of confusion. But how much confusion do we hear on an hourly basis coming from that one-eyed monster called the TV or the pervasiveness of social media? How do we disconnect from this daily programming of the media? All we hear is one death after another, and you mean to tell me we should not be affected? When will we have all forms of media telling the good news about what's really going on? I understand that good news doesn't sell as well as bad news, but constant bad news is destructive to the human spirit.

Let's talk about the effects that negative news has on the conscious mind and the subconscious. First of all, the subconscious stores the bad news, and most people don't have the skills to delete bad information. The mind is like a field; when we allow negative news to linger too long, we grow intolerant. Some people blame the devil for everything. However, I blame constant exposure to bad information. I would compare bad information to poison. What else should we expect from the great minds that God created? Americans need to raise a new vision and change the way we use fear as a controlling tool to destroy young minds before they get a chance to grow.

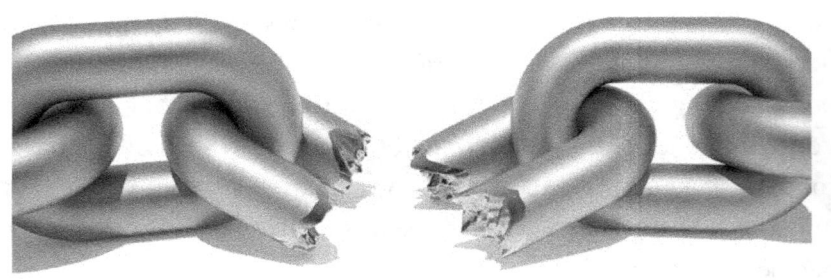

One Bad Link Will Break a Chain

One Bad Link
Will Break a Chain   <small>Chapter XXXIII</small>

When I was a kid, I was called "Mr. Fix It." Once I tried to take three junk bicycles and build one good bike. First, I made sure I had two good tires and handlebars for one bike. But when I got to the V chain, something happened. I tried to fix the chain, so I took links from one chain trying to make a chain that would fit perfectly. However, when I got to the last link, I took a hammer and closed the final link. Now it was time to try out my new bike. All the kids in the neighborhood were laughing and saying things like, "Jeff built a bike, but I bet you, it won't work, right!" To tell you the truth, they were right. As soon as I took off, the chain broke. I soon realized that when building a bike, you can't use weak links in the chain.

With that being said, why does America use so many weak links? In America we allow weak links to hang around too long instead of fixing the problem. We allow them to become bigger problems. Let's take a look at poverty. Poverty is a weak link in the chain. When we allow poverty to hang around, it affects the entire chain. It will shut down the program, like my piecework shut down my program as a child when I was building my bike. Some people in America would rather cut poverty off like the doctor would cut out cancer from someone's body. But human beings are involved. So how strong is America? I hate to tell the President and those in the House and Senate: America is only as strong as its weakest link. America, it's time to include all in the process of building a great nation! We can no longer forget the weakest links. When I was in the military, we used to run three and four miles. Sometimes after about three miles, some of us would start falling out of the run instead of leaving the slower runners behind. We had a couple of super runners. They would go back and get the ones that fell out. Sometimes the entire company would turn around because the leader of the company was determined not to leave anyone behind. This was called teamwork, and teamwork makes the dream work.

I believe America has to do a better job of policing the weak. For

One Bad Link
Will Break a Chain

years we as a nation have only reached out to the strong. We have talent shows to find the best, as if the rest is no good. We need to stop looking for the highest G.P.A.'s. I'm not saying a high G.P.A is not important, but look at Enron. Those white-collar criminals had high G.P.A's but didn't have character. Let's fix the link that keeps breaking the chain.

For example, our health care is finally getting fixed, thanks to President Barack Obama. Mr. Obama, thank you for considering the poor. Once again, if you read this book, I think you would make a great world leader. Seventy-five percent of the world's people like you. I think you have the power to transform Africa for the better. Maybe you would consider moving to Kenya and becoming a world leader from Kenya because some in America have not given you all the respect that you truly deserve. But you would be well received in the motherland. Could it be possible that God created you to deliver your own people? But America had you for eight years preparing you for your true calling. Mr. Obama, I know deep down inside you crave change, but America, or should I say some, don't want change. It's been a long time coming but a change is going to come. So I say to you; yes, we can, when the House says "no." I say, " Yes, we can." It's time to get the fire back in this nation that we once had when you first ran for President. Yes, we can!

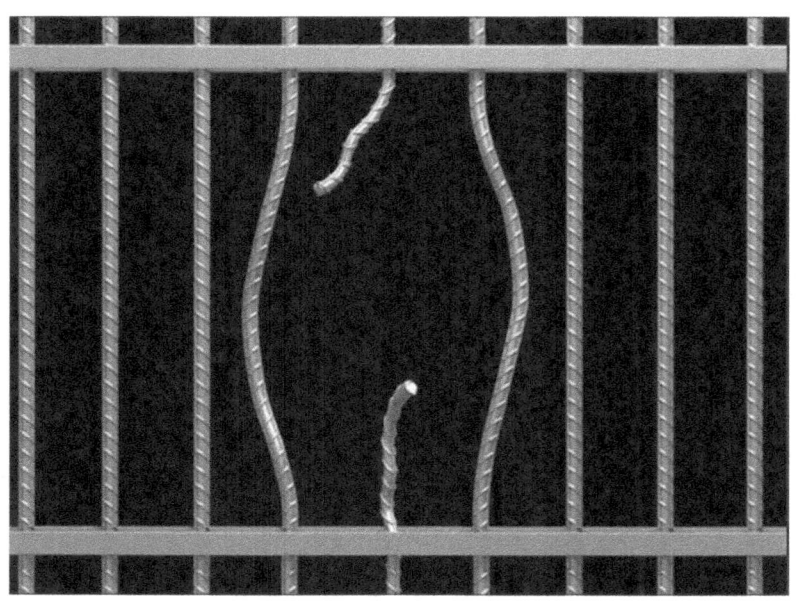

CHAPTER XXXIV

Break Out of Prison Now

It's time to come out of that dark cell that has held you captive too many years. Yes, you have been depressed too long, and life is about to pass you by. Man, woman or child, you were born for greatness, but you have allowed restrictions to block you from your divine destiny. No, you are not a loser. Your so-called friends may have told you that you were a loser, but losers can become winners. If you still have a mind to win, you can win. I don't care what you have been through. I can find thousands that have been through a lot more and made it, so make up your mind once and for all. No more gloomy days; no more distractions or sadness. If you are not happy, it's your own fault. Make yourself happy; you deserve to be happy. I know it's hard to see your way right now. But the sun is still shining; it's just being hidden by the clouds. I had many dark days also, but I decided to write my way out of despair. I believe all things are possible.

I once was an alcoholic, and my mind was very cloudy. But thanks to my Lord and Savior Jesus Christ, I am nineteen years clean. I was in prison in my mind, but for such a time as this, I was called to shine the light on those who want to be free. Freedom starts in the mind. The Bible says that Satan is the author of confusion (1 Cor. 14:33). Yes, his goal is to hold all of us captive in our minds, so that we can't fulfill our God-given destinies. Joyce Myers wrote a book called The Battlefield of the Mind, "Yes, the battle is fought in the mind, but we become a prisoner of the mind when we stop fighting the battle."

Three Things You Can't Hide:
The Sun, The Moon and the Truth

Three things you can't hide: The sun, The Moon and The Truth

One thing about the sun is that the sun affects everything in the solar system in some way or another. The sun causes things to grow; it provides heat on a cold day. Also, it's a big ball of energy. The sun impressed the Africans in ancient times to the point that they made a God out of it. With this being said, man cannot live without the sun. The sun is light, and light cannot be hidden. When it's dark on one side of the globe, it's light on the other. When the sun is reflecting on the other side of the earth, the moon is shining from the reflections of the sun. The truth shall always shine through, no matter how many lies we have in our heads. The truth will make us free. The truth is that light shining through the darkness, but the problem is that most people have lived in darkness for so long. When the truth comes, some would rather continue living lies because it seems too expensive to make that change. Also, most of us would rather believe a lie over the truth. Som people choose darkness over light because light exposes all of our weal spots. However, we should want our weak spots exposed, so that we can allow God to make us strong in those areas. In the Bible there is a verse that says, "Men shall reap what they sow" (Gal. 6:7). That means, good or bad, no matter how many lies have been sown, the truth will eventually show up, and the truth can't be hidden, even though many have tried.

The late Dr. Martin Luther King Jr. once said, "No lie can live forever." Why? Because a lie can only hide until the truth shows up, just like you can walk in darkness until the morning. Just like clockwork here comes the sun to bring light. Always remember the three things that can't be hidden: the sun, moon and truth.

This is how the truth works. When the truth shows up, first of all, we all have to make a decision or some decisions. Do I continue to walk in this lie, or do I change? Did I say change? Yes, I said change. People who hate change will waste most of their lives walking in darkness. I started writing five years ago because it was time to change. I had been in this darkness too long; it was time for Jeff Hairston to walk in the light with all of my short- comings. Yes, I have many, but I am sorry. I am ready to walk out onto the stage and sing my song and speak my truth. No more fear; it's my time to shine!

CHAPTER XXXVI

Be Encouraged

We live in a society where there are a lot of uncertain days. The world economy is in a very slow recovery. Since I was raised in a family of ten children, I can relate to the have-nots. However, be encouraged, no matter what you are going through.

You can make it if you try. Just take courage, my friend; better days are ahead of you. Take a look back over your life and see from where God brought you. In the words of President Obama, "Yes, you have what it takes to make that change." You have a great mind. Every day you are getting better. No one can stop you now. You can be anything you want to be and do anything you want. Your future is bright.

People like you; people respect you. Your best days are ahead. It's not too late, and you are not too old. Don't give up on your dreams; don't let the storms of life stop you from reaching your destiny. Here are some keys to reaching your full potential:

You must have a made up mind. You must be free from the dark prison cell mentality. Your mind must be transformed and renewed in order to process your God-given potential.

You must have auto progression; that means to keep speaking what you want to see until it manifests. You must speak those things that are not as though they are. You must have a burning desire and continue to maintain this burning desire. You must have a strong thirst and desire because Scripture says that God will give us the desires of the heart.

If you operate from these principals, then your mind will be free from the prison mind. Therefore, you can walk in the direction of your destiny. Life is too short to allow your mind to defeat you any longer. Come on, your life is not over until they roll you down the aisle. Why are you allowing the enemy to talk you out of your future? I know you have been listening to him. The enemy has been telling you it's over; he's saying things like you don't have what it takes!

CHAPTER XXXVII

Trapped at Christmas Time

Trapped at
Christmas Time   Chapter XXXVII

I was talking to the lady at Avis Rental Car on December 23rd. She asked me if I was ready for Christmas. I replied yes; I am ready because I don't have children. Her response was that we have about twelve grands, and then I started thinking about how stressful that could be on a person's mind, wondering how to make all those children smile on Christmas day.

Christmas has to be the most stressful season because we have forgotten what the season is all about. Homer wrote once that when the legends die, it will be the result of people no longer believing in them. Have you ever felt trapped in your mind at Christmas, or has depression tried to creep up on you because you allow the pressure of trying to please everyone? I have come to set your mind free. Yes, Santa Claus is just a legend, and society has used Santa to control the masses of the people. But my question to you is: When will you wake up and walk out of that trap? It's time to relieve yourself of that responsibility. Sit those children down and tell them the truth about Christmas. This will be the last year you will be participating in the rat race.

I watch people spend their light bill money or even their rent money trying to please their children. Some parents will take out loans or may use their credit cards trying to make everyone happy. Do you see the trap? The trap is designed to bog your household down in a bundle of debt, so that you can spend the next couple of years trying to dig your way out of that trap. Then, here comes Christmas again.

Please don't get upset with the messenger. I am just trying to speak some truth to all of these lies. Christmas is not the time to stress yourself to the point of suicide. I can remember that when I was a child, mom and dad would spend their life savings to make sure our Christmas tree was loaded down and was I happy to wake up on Christmas morning. Yes, I was very happy. But take a minute and think about those families who are less fortunate and are trying to impress the kid. My mom

Trapped at
Christmas Time

and dad were only trying to keep up with the tradition of Christmas. I'm not saying there's anything wrong with the birth of Christ, but I have a problem with watching the system continue to entrap the mind of the masses, especially the poor. Ask yourself this question: When will I break this cycle of poverty? Wasting all of your hard earned money on the toys and electronics definitely is not how you should be spelling relief.

I'm Coming Out

I'm Coming Out

Until you have seen the darkness of prison, you will never be able to appreciate the light of walking in freedom. For years, I have been in prison, not in a physical holding cell but a mental holding cell. I have been clean for nineteen years from drinking alcohol and doing drugs. But I just discovered why I was drunk for so long. I took my first drink when I was thirteen years of age. I can remember that first drink just like it was yesterday. I felt so good, but I noticed something else. I didn't feel depression anymore. I was drinking because I was depressed as a child. I decree to myself that I'm coming out with my hands up. I'm free at last; free at last!

Married and Lonely

Married and Lonely

Unless we deal with the internal struggles, we will walk down the aisle and make a vow that can become a yoke of bondage. Since I have been married for twenty-eight years and have experienced some ups and downs, I feel that I can share some strengths and hopes. First of all, two wounded people being joined together spells disaster. The pastor needs to do a better job of counseling young people and trying to prepare them for the struggles of life. What we do is march people down the aisle, but we don't tell them that around fifty, the man or woman may go through the change of life. Depression may set in. What will you do? Will you try to escape through alcoholism or drugs? Maybe you will walk out the door looking for relief in another man or woman. If a man or a woman can't deal with whom his or her parents were, he or she will carry that dysfunction into the marriage. For instance, what if Daddy was a male whore?

The man can trace that spirit, and nine times out of ten, the son will be tempted to chase everything in a dress. On the other hand, if the mother was free-spirited and gave her goods to every Tom, Dick, and Harry, then the daughter may be faithful for a short period of time before temptation tries to pull her out the door.

I can talk about Jeff Hairston. I got married at the age of twenty-three. Before I got married, I was a whore, and after getting married, I was a whore. I was born to two married people, and I'm confessing that all my life I have wrestled with a whoring spirit. Nobody wants to talk about it, but most men really, especially African-Americans, struggle with being faithful to one woman. Take a look around just in case you have not seen the struggle.

However, the struggle didn't just start. Look at the Bible: Abraham, the father of many nations, couldn't contain himself (Genesis 16:4). I mean Abraham was God's man, but he loved the opposite sex. Take a look at Solomon; the man had one thousand women (Kings 11:3)! We live in a realistic world, but most of us love to hide stuff and sweep it all under the rug. I will be the first to say that marriage is very good when two people decide to hold to their vows, and that's what we should tell young people. Yes, we still get lonely as married people. But my question to you is, "How will you spell relief after you get married?" I spelled it with alcohol and sometimes extra-marital affairs, depression and overeating.

This will go down in history as the most transparent book you will ever read. I am hoping that my honesty will help some young person deal with his or her drama before he or she walks down the aisle and messes up someone else's life.

I want to take this time to thank my wife Cynthia for marrying a man like me. I am saved today, but I am an honest Christian, saved but struggling every day to be a good man. I heard Dr. Mike Murdock say, "Struggle means I have not yet been conquered." My favorite song is "I've had some good days; I've had some hills to climb." All of my good days outweigh my bad days. I won't complain. If I don't call on Jesus every day of my life, I would go back to drinking or go back to running women. I need Jesus like a drunk needs a drink. I need him like a crackhead needs a fix. Thank you, Lord, for saving a sinner like me!

If I can make it, anybody can make it. Don't give up when you get lonely; don't give up when you feel the temptation to walk out. Hang in there when it gets hard.

www.ingramcontent.com/pod-product-compliance
Lightning Source LLC
Chambersburg PA
CBHW070154290526
45789CB00002B/766